The Planning *of*
Center City Philadelphia:

from William Penn
to the Present

Essay by John Andrew Gallery

Includes five walking tours

Published by the Center for Architecture, Inc.
Philadelphia, Pennsylvania 19103

THE PLANNING OF CENTER CITY
PHILADELPHIA: FROM WILLIAM
PENN TO THE PRESENT

PUBLISHED BY THE CENTER FOR
ARCHITECTURE
PHILADELPHIA, PENNSYLVANIA 19103

ISBN 0-9793787-0-2

PRINTED AND BOUND IN THE
UNITED STATES

DESIGN BY JOEL KATZ DESIGN
ASSOCIATES

TYPOGRAPHY BY DUKE & COMPANY

PRINTED BY CENVEO PRESS

CONTENTS

Thomas Holme's plan
of the Province of
Pennsylvania

1687

4

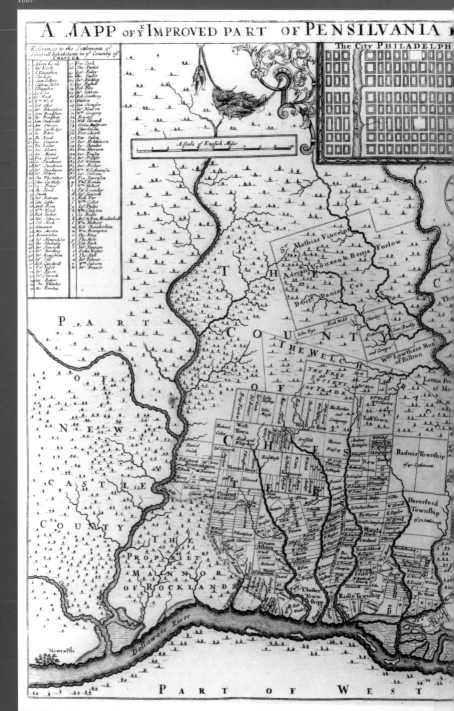

The Planning *of*
Center City Philadelphia

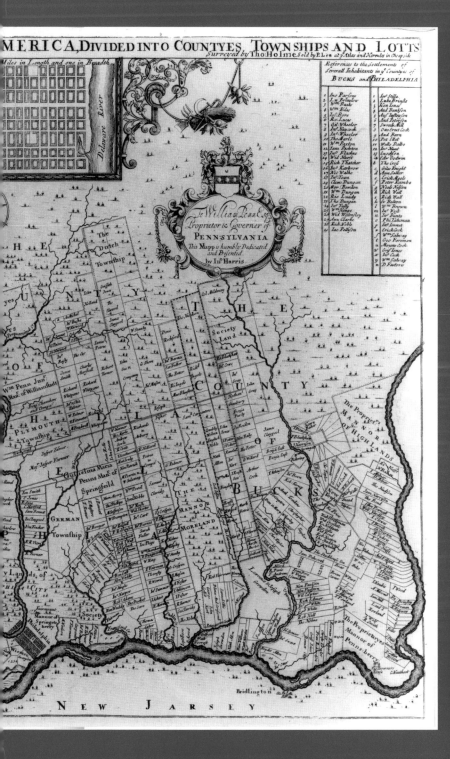

When the colony of Pennsylvania was founded in 1682, the city of Philadelphia consisted of the area between the Delaware and Schuylkill rivers, and the present day Vine Street and South Street. The plan for the city designed by William Penn and his surveyor Thomas Holme guided its growth from a modest settlement to the most distinguished city in the colonies at the time of the American Revolution.

William Penn's Treaty with the Indians

1684

Benjamin West

Philadelphia was the first phase in Penn's plan for the development of the colony of Pennsylvania—a 45,000-square-mile area given to Penn by King Charles II in exchange for a debt owed Penn's father, an admiral in the king's service. Penn envisioned selling land in the colony in a controlled manner. He intended to establish a town center with surrounding agricultural land and once that had been sufficiently populated, to open up land to the west for an additional town center supported by agricultural land. Thus, from the outset, Philadelphia had two distinct components: a city with a formal plan to guide its growth and a surrounding countryside of agricultural settlement and country estates with no plan at all.

In spite of Penn's intentions, settlement extended outward beyond the city limits into the adjacent countryside from the very first. By 1854, the population of the countryside was double that of the city and the developed area so extensive and so lacking in basic services, that the city and the surrounding county were consolidated into one political unit—the 135-square-mile city of Philadelphia as we know it today. Although civic and political leaders created some plans to guide the growth of this larger area, most planning efforts have focused on the original city, now known as Center City. Here can be found the results of plans influenced by the City Beautiful movement in the late 19th and early 20th centuries and ambitious plans proposed in the 1920s, but largely implemented in the period from 1950 to 1970 when Philadelphia was acknowledged as a leader in city planning in this country.

The history of planning in Center City Philadelphia reflects the periods and types of planning that occurred in other older cities in the United States. Although it begins with one man's vision, it is the story of the collective vision of many men and women—civic leaders and professional planners—acting most often through civic associations to express their vision of a city both beautiful and practical, with varying degrees of interest and support from city government. This is a brief account of that planning history and the key individuals whose vision helped shape Center City Philadelphia into the distinctive place it is today.

Penn Patent to Samuel Carpenter

1684

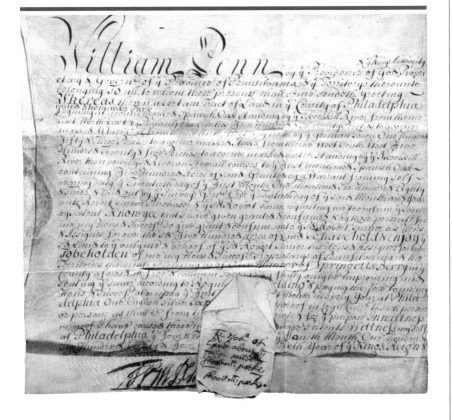

WILLIAM PENN'S AND THOMAS HOLME'S PLAN FOR PHILADELPHIA

1682–1701

William Penn

1644–1718

Some of the South and Eastbounds of Pennsylvania

1681

John Thornton and John Seller

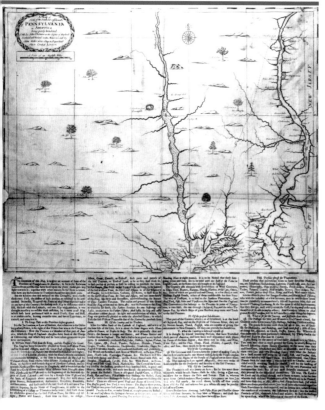

The colony of Pennsylvania and the city of Philadelphia were founded by William Penn. Penn's interest in establishing a colony in the New World was a reflection of the two quite different aspects of his life. Penn was raised as an aristocrat; he inherited estates from his father, an admiral in the service of the king, and acquired further property and wealth through his first marriage. He attended court and was a good friend of the king's brother, the Duke of York, the future King James II. But Penn was also a member of the Religious Society of Friends (Quakers), one of the most oppressed religious sects in England at the time. He was an important religious leader, author of many books and pamphlets on Quaker issues, and spent time in jail for his religious beliefs.

Penn's interest in establishing a colony grew out of these two distinctly different interests: as a religious leader he wanted to provide a refuge for Quakers and others to be free of the religious persecution they experienced in England in the 1600s. And he also wanted to make money and increase his wealth.

In 1677, Penn helped other Quakers settle the western portion of New Jersey. The experience convinced him that colonization might be a profitable venture. This led him to seek a grant of land from the king, in exchange for a debt owed his father. In 1681, he was granted a charter by King Charles II for 45,000 square miles of land—the largest grant of land given to an individual—named Pennsylvania by the king in honor of Penn's father.

To make his colony a successful business venture, Penn had to attract settlers. To do so he had to offer incentives that would influence settlers to come to Pennsylvania rather than to New Jersey or other colonies. Religious freedom was a strong incentive, but land was the key to Penn's success.

At the time, it was very difficult for the average person to own any significant amount of land in England. Penn envisioned his colony as an agriculturally based settlement where large tracts of land would be available and affordable. His land offering reflected this. To those who would purchase land first, he offered 100 shares each consisting of 5,000 acres in the rich agricultural countryside surrounding Philadelphia, 100 acres in what were called Liberty Lands surrounding the commercial center, and two acres in the commercial center or city. He did not expect many to buy 5,000 acres so each share was allowed to be subdivided among multiple purchasers. All told, Penn sold slightly more than 500,000 acres to 657 First Purchasers, the majority of whom purchased fewer than 700 acres each. This was a huge amount of land compared to what would have been possible to obtain in England.

Penn appointed Thomas Holme as his surveyor general. Holme was a Quaker businessman from Ireland who had experience as a land surveyor, and who had purchased land and was about to move to Pennsylvania when Penn appointed him. Penn sent him ahead to lay out the property he had sold and was in the process of selling. His directions to Holme were quite general: he knew he wanted the commercial center located where there would be a good port, but he had no specific idea about the form it should take. He knew he wanted the residential areas to be a "green Country towne" not like the densely built up city of London he knew and disliked. He thought that each residential lot should be approximately 825 feet wide and have a river view. Needless to say, that was impractical—it would have resulted in a settlement consisting of country estates stretching 16 miles along the Delaware River.

Penn assumed the site of the commercial center or city would be at present-day Chester. But there were already too many settlers there, so Thomas Holme and others Penn had sent ahead to establish the government of the colony selected a different site for the city at the narrow point between the Delaware and Schuylkill rivers. Holme could only purchase 200 acres from Swedish settlers (purchase from existing settlers was a requirement of Penn's charter and part of his policy of dealing fairly with Swedish settlers and Native Americans). He began to lay out lots in a plan that extended west as far as what is now 4th Street. Before he could finish, Penn arrived and realized this area was too small to allow for future expansion. He purchased more land and extended the plan to the Schuylkill River, enlarging the city to 1,200 acres.

There is no way to know how the plan of Philadelphia was created or even who was its true author, Penn or Holme. Much can be said in Holme's favor. He was a surveyor, he was familiar with settlements that had been established by Oliver Cromwell in Ireland, and he is thought to have known Londonderry,

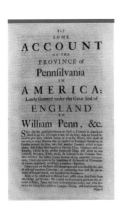

Penn's description of Pennsylvania
1681

whose plan bears similarities to the plan of Philadelphia. Penn, on the other hand, had traveled in France and may have seen recent settlements there, and most likely knew Richard Newcourt's plan for rebuilding London after the great fire of 1666, also thought to have been a possible influence on the plan of Philadelphia. Whatever the truth, the plan was created and published in 1683. It consisted of a grid of streets, with a major north/south and east/west street each much larger than all others. A public park or square was located in each quadrant and a center square for public buildings placed at the intersection of the two major streets. Within the grid of streets one-acre and one-half-acre lots were laid out equally on the Delaware and Schuylkill riverfronts so that the city would grow in toward the center and increase the value of land owned there by Penn. The plan of major streets and public parks in Center City today differs only from the plan of 1683 in the location of Broad Street, which was moved farther west after Holme found the exact location of the high point between the two rivers.

Although a plan for the town was important to enable lots to be assigned on which houses could be built, more important was the subdivision of land in the surrounding agricultural countryside. This is

Plan of Londonderry and Newcourt's plan for London

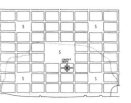

Thomas Holme's plan of the city of Philadelphia

1683

where the large parcels land were located that provided the incentive for settlers to come to Pennsylvania. Holme's map of 1687 (see pages 4–5) shows the subdivision of this broader area and gives a good understanding of the magnitude of the undertaking. The map shows the 500,000 acres of land in the countryside with the names of First Purchasers, the Liberty Lands and the rather small-by-comparison 1,200-acre city at the edge of this area, adjacent to the Delaware River. Penn assumed that the city of Philadelphia would always be surrounded by an agricultural countryside. This is the pattern he knew in England and Ireland, which he assumed would endure. Therefore, he saw no need to provide a plan for this surrounding area as specific as the plan for the city. Thus, from the outset Pennsylvania consisted of two different places: a city with a formal plan that provided a framework within which residential, commercial and institutional uses would develop, and a surrounding countryside with no plan at all, consisting of huge tracts of agricultural land connected by a road system so informal it is not even indicated on Holme's 1687 map.

Settlement over this vast area began very quickly in part due to the Quaker form of worship. While Pilgrims in New England had to be within walking or riding distance of a church for Sunday services, Quakers did not require specific religious buildings as places for worship and could, and did, meet in small groups in individual homes.

Penn spent relatively little time in his colony. He came in 1682–84 to establish the plan and again in 1699–1701. During the latter period he created the Charter of Privileges that established a form of governance for the colony that incorporated freedom of worship and many other legal rights not generally available in England. It would later influence the U.S. Constitution. Although he turned over the governance of the colony to the colonists, he—and after his death in 1718, his wife and his sons—retained ownership of all undeveloped land in Philadelphia and Pennsylvania until the American Revolution.

THE COLONIAL CITY
1701 to 1800

Developed area in 1776

Although Penn consulted with many individuals he hoped would invest in Pennsylvania while he prepared his land offering, his plan for Philadelphia lacked a critical ingredient that would confront future city planners and become one of the critical planning issues of the mid-20th century. Penn failed to include what we would today call a citizen participation component in the development of his plan. It quickly became apparent that early settlers found many of the assumptions underlying the clear and orderly plan devised for the city of Philadelphia to be inappropriate. And so, from the first, colonists made changes to the plan that Penn did not approve but could not prevent.

Three assumptions in particular found little favor with the first settlers. First, Penn assumed that settlement would begin on both riverfronts and move inward. But no one wanted to live on the Schuylkill River, which was separated from the port on the Delaware River by forest that would not be entirely cleared for 100 years. Penn eventually assigned these lots to investors who remained in London and located the lots of all those who were ready to move to Philadelphia along the Delaware River. Consequently, settlement began here and only slowly moved westward.

Second, although the lots in the town were only one or one-half acres, they were still viewed as being too large. Typical lots were 100 feet wide and nearly 400 feet deep, meaning that houses were separated from one another by large areas of forest. While this certainly gave the feeling of a "green Country towne" it gave no sense of community nor did it provide the proximity sought by settlers in a foreign wilderness. Consequently, property owners began to divide their land into smaller lots and to build houses to rent to the large number of settlers who poured into Philadelphia in the early 1700s. This required the introduction of intermediary alleys and streets between the major streets of the Penn/Holme plan. The area between Front and Second streets is a good example of these modifications. Holme originally laid out 43 lots between Front and Second, Market and Race streets. By as early as 1698 there were 70 lots and by 1702 there were 102, along with a series of alleys to provide access. Elfreth's Alley (see Old City Tour) is an excellent example of this type of subdivision and associated development.

Lastly, Penn did not realize the importance of the relationship to the river. In his early concepts he proposed that all lots have a river view. While the view was not mandatory to early settlers, proximity to the port was. Consequently, rather than grow east to west within the legal boundaries of the city as Penn hoped, settlement grew north and south along the

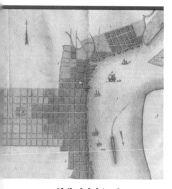

Philadelphia along the Delaware River

1774
Luigi Castiglioni

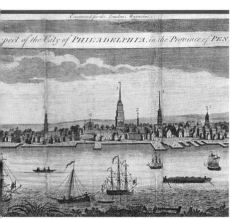

East Prospect of the City of Philadelphia

1750–54

Nicholas Scull

river, into the Liberty Lands outside the city boundaries. Although the grid plan of streets of the city was often extended into these areas, there was no requirement to do so. Consequently the street plans for Southwark (now Queen Village) south of the city and Frankford and Northern Liberties to the north exhibit irregularities not found in Center City.

For the first few years settlement of the area now known as Old City (Front to 5th streets, Vine to Walnut streets) grew slowly as buildable lots were carved out of the forest and adapted to the terrain of creeks, hills and ponds that actually existed, in contrast to the apparently flat site of Holme's plan. However, Philadelphia prospered and in a very short time presented an impressive prospect along the Delaware River for arriving settlers who steadily came to Pennsylvania in the early 1700s. By 1740, the city population had grown to 10,000—second only to Boston. The plan provided a loose framework of streets within which development took place. Most people worked out of their homes so businesses and residences were totally intermixed. Freedom of worship attracted all religious denominations and churches took their place among the businesses and homes.

Penn's designation of the center square as the place for public buildings also failed to recognize how

Imaginary view of Philadelphia

1702

slowly the city would grow westward. A Quaker meetinghouse was briefly located there, but the area around 2nd and Market streets quickly became the site of public buildings and the heart of the city. Here were located the major markets for the city (closely connected to the port), the Courthouse and town hall, the Great Quaker Meetinghouse, the jail, and the principal Anglican church.

By 1765, the mixture of business and residence in Old City, as well as a population that had grown to 25,000, led more affluent families to seek housing to the south in what is now Society Hill. Here the mix of business with residences was less, but there was still diversity. Rich families with large mansions lived right next door to their servants and slaves in small houses. There was neither land use nor economic segregation in the colonial city.

Although this growth took place with the framework of Penn's plan, decisions about development were not made in a manner that was planned to influence a particular pattern or direction of growth or distribution of activities. New housing could fill in land within the street grid, but when institutions needed larger parcels of land they were forced to go to the edge of the city into the undeveloped areas west of 4th Street. When a new site was sought for government buildings in 1729, land was purchased at 5th and Chestnut streets because it was on the edge of the city where a large undeveloped parcel could be obtained. For the same reason Pennsylvania Hospital located at 8th and Spruce streets in 1755. These decisions promoted further western growth, but not in a deliberate manner.

By the time of the American Revolution, the population of the city had reached 35,000. Development had expanded west as far as 5th Street; streets were paved and lit, and hundreds of houses were available to own or rent. Society Hill contained large mansions of the wealthy, and there was an abundance of civic, religious and social institutions. Philadelphia in 1776 was the most distinguished urban settlement in the colonies.

Although Penn's plan was the official framework for growth, a careful observer would have seen a very different pattern of urban structure than Holme's plan of 1683 implied. Standing at the heart of the city at 2nd and Market streets looking west, it would have been apparent that the structure of settlement was based upon a series of radial roads extending in all directions. These stopped at the edge of the city where the grid of streets was mandatory, but once beyond those artificial lines a radiating pattern of roads extended north to Frankford, northwest to Germantown, southwest through Southwark and what is now South Philadelphia, west via Market Street and

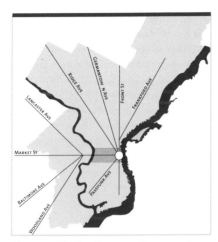

Diagram of Regional Roads

Lancaster, Haverford, Chester and Baltimore avenues once past the Schuylkill River. These were the paths that connected the extensive settlements outside the city limits to the city itself. In the 1700s they provided the true framework of the larger region and were the routes along which major commercial development occurred through the 19th century.

American independence and the formation of a new nation had a significant impact on Philadelphia. All of the land owned by the Penn family became the property of the state. Much was sold off quickly to pay war debts. Although Penn's plan was retained, the sale of land in the city led to further subdivision and the introduction of even more small streets and alleys. At the time, they promoted crowding and congestion; today they are among the most charming streets and residential settings in Center City. Sale of Liberty Lands north of the city promoted the development of new housing and fostered continued growth of townships outside the city limits. Nonetheless, by 1790, when the first U.S. Census counted the population of the Philadelphia area at 53,000, the city was still concentrated north and south along the Delaware River and had not expanded much farther west than 7th Street.

Plan of Philadelphia and its Environs

1796

John Hills

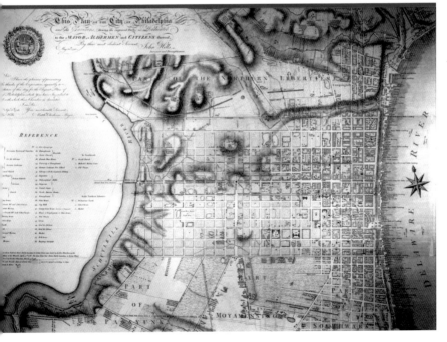

Developed area in 1800

Penn's concept of a central city surrounded by a rural countryside remained substantially intact through the end of the 18th century. But in the early decades of the 19th century, important changes began to take place. The most significant, the ones that would shape the future growth of Philadelphia, took place outside the boundaries of the city. Water-powered mills had already started to locate and encourage rapid growth in such places as Kensington, Spring Garden and Moyamensing. The invention of the steam engine in 1803 allowed factories to be located anywhere and become larger than water-powered mills. New manufacturing companies like the Baldwin Locomotive Works, with 3,000 employees, attracted an influx of immigrants to the city and encouraged the development of block after block of worker housing within their immediate areas. The result was a more socially diverse population, spread over a much larger geographic area. By 1840, the majority of the 250,000 residents lived outside the city in areas that had once been rural farmland.

While the most extensive changes occurred in the countryside, the city changed substantially as well. The shift in focus from 2nd and Market streets to 5th and Chestnut streets that had begun with the construction of the Pennsylvania State House in 1732–48 was reinforced when the State House and adjacent buildings served as the capital of the United States, the location of Congress and the Supreme Court. After the capital was moved from Philadelphia, the use of these buildings by the Pennsylvania Assembly and the Philadelphia city government continued to encourage businesses, banks, law firms and others to move into the immediate area. This shift in focus was not a planned decision, but it influenced the pattern of growth of Center City for the next 100 years. Although the port continued to be important and stretched up and down the river, manufacturing business grew steadily within the city limits. Industrialization separated places of business and work, and for the first time sections of the city became exclusively residential or exclusively commercial. The fashionable neighborhoods became those newly developed between 10th and Broad streets. The older areas east of 7th Street deteriorated as a result of overcrowding by steadily arriving immigrants. New houses were larger and built speculatively, but not in a continuous pattern. Large areas of open space continued to exist east of Broad Street, and although the forest had been completely cleared to the Schuylkill River by 1800, even as late as 1840 the area west from Broad Street to the Schuylkill River was still largely undeveloped.

By 1854, the growth of population and development outside the city was so extensive, and the lack

Developed area in 1850

of services—particularly police and fire—so great, the city of Philadelphia as defined by William Penn and the surrounding Philadelphia County were consolidated into one legal entity constituting the 135-square-mile city of Philadelphia as it exists today. This consolidation extended the powers of government previously limited to the city into the surrounding areas. The street grid of the city was extended with little regard for the radial regional roads that had formed the structure of transportation and commercial development. Consolidation also provided the impetus for two actions that would have significant impact on the future of Center City.

One of the powers granted to the new city government was the ability to acquire land for public open space, prompting development of a plan to protect the city's water supply, an issue of great concern. In 1812, the city had purchased land on Faire Mount for construction of the city water works and later, in 1828, purchased additional land to protect the water supply. Fairmount Park was founded in 1855 when the Lemon Hill estate was dedicated as a public park.

View of Fairmount Water Works

c. 1838

J. T. Bowden

In 1856, additional land was acquired and in 1859 the firm of Sidney & Adams was retained to develop a landscape plan for the area immediately north of the waterworks. By 1867, it was recognized that public parks were important not only to protect the water supply, but to provide a place for residents to escape the density of the industrial city. The Fairmount Park Commission was established to manage the park and in 1868 the park was greatly enlarged on both the east and west sides of the Schuylkill River, including the acquisition of 1,800 acres in the Wissahickon Valley.

It is probably accurate to say that the creation of

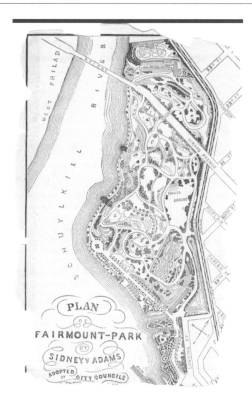

Plan for Fairmount Park
1859
Sidney & Adams

Fairmount Park was the first act of planning since the work of William Penn and Thomas Holme and the engineers hired by the Fairmount Park Commission to plan and develop the park might be considered the first city planners of the modern era. Although the park was located outside the boundaries of the original city, it would have an important influence on the planning of Center City in the late-19th and early-20th centuries.

As important as the creation of the park was, the decision that would have the greatest influence on the future form of Center City was not a planned decision, but the result of a public referendum. Although the city had only grown as far west as 10th Street by the 1830s, real estate developers and businessmen wanted to encourage westward expansion. In 1838, a group proposed the construction of new municipal buildings on Center Square, the site set aside for such purpose by William Penn. When the city and county were consolidated in 1854, there was a necessary and rapid expansion of government services and court activities to serve what was now a city with more than double its previous population. As a result, city offices expanded into buildings in the entire area around Independence Hall. The dispersion of city government among many buildings revived the idea of a new municipal building. A competition for the design of a building on Center Square was won by architect John McArthur, Jr. in 1860. Delayed by the Civil War, a second competition was held in 1869—also won by McArthur—this time for a mu-

Model of proposed City Hall on Independence Square
1860
John McArthur, Jr., architect

nicipal complex on Independence Square. Public outcry at the demolition of historic buildings and the impact on Independence Hall (perhaps the first expression of public interest in historic preservation) led the state legislature to intervene and hold a public referendum to choose whether the new building should be on Washington Square or Center Square. Center Square was selected by a vote of roughly 50,000 to 30,000. McArthur was selected as architect. He was assisted by Thomas U. Walter, architect of the U.S. Capitol Building, who brought in Alexander Milne Calder to develop a sculptural program for the building. Construction began in 1871, with the cornerstone laid in 1874. Occupancy of the building actually began in 1877 while it was still under construction, but the building was not considered finished until 1901. Its most dramatic feature is the 491-foot-high tower, the tallest masonry structure in the world, on top of which is a statue of William Penn.

City Hall did not lead the movement west, but it solidified the trend. By 1860, most of Philadelphia's elite families were moving west of Broad Street toward Rittenhouse Square. In the last decade of the 19th century and the first decade of the 20th century major commercial buildings followed, spurred by the construction of City Hall. By the beginning of the 20th century, the financial and business center of the city had moved from 5th and Chestnut streets to South Broad Street where it would remain until the mid-1900s.

City Hall under construction

1880s

THE PARKWAY AND THE BEGINNING OF MODERN CITY PLANNING
1880–1920

Developed area in 1900

For 200 years after William Penn and Thomas Holme created the plan of Philadelphia, there was nothing that could be called city planning in the sense that we understand it today. During the 18th and 19th centuries, the development and growth of the city were the result of the actions of private developers and property owners. However, by the late 1800s, individual citizens and civic organizations began to express concern about the form the city was taking.

Although city planning was not acknowledged as a professional activity until the beginning of the 20th century—the first national conference on city planning was held in 1909—a concern for city planning in the United States is thought to have started at the end of the century following the 1893 Columbian World's Exposition in Chicago. The exposition provided an impetus for planning in Philadelphia, just

Columbian World's Exposition, Chicago
1893

as it did for many other American cities. But in Philadelphia modern city planning actually began somewhat earlier.

Beginning in the 1870s, engineers working for the Fairmount Park Commission and other individuals began to advocate for a system of diagonal roads that would link what they felt had become a fragmented city. Earliest among these was Lewis Haupt, a civil engineer for the Park Commission, who was the first to suggest that a pattern of diagonal streets be superimposed over the grid of the city. Over the next 50 years this idea would be advocated by many others. In the 1890s, the women's Civic Club sponsored a series of lectures on city planning by Albert Kelsey and others. Kelsey, too, advocated for the idea of diagonal boulevards, as did Bernard Haldeman, head of the General Plans Division of the City's Bureau of Surveys, perhaps the first governmental city planning department. Haldeman would later become one of the charter members of the American City Planning Institute. Andrew Wright Crawford, secretary of the influential City Parks Association, lent his support in 1901, and in 1902 Frank Miles Day, a prominent architect, developed a plan for South Philadelphia based on a system of diagonal boulevards.

This interest in diagonal boulevards linking different parts of the city coincided with proposals for connecting City Hall and Fairmount Park. The expansion and consolidation of Fairmount Park that

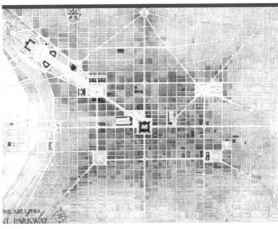

Proposal for diagonal boulevards
1917
Jacques Greber

had occurred by 1868 led John Penington & Son to publish a pamphlet in 1871 urging that a connection be made between the park and Broad Street. The unknown author, perhaps one of the park engineers, stated: "If the great park, with which we have undertaken to adorn the city, is to be a place of general resort and to benefit all of our citizens, it must be brought within the reach of all."

The proposed solution was to create two new boulevards on and near Callowhill Street that would connect the park to Broad Street. In 1884, Charles Landis, the developer of Vineland, New Jersey, went further. Landis proposed a diagonal "grand avenue" from City Hall, which was then under construction on Center Square, to the foot of Faire Mount, where the city reservoir was located and Fairmount Park began. A group of prominent citizens supported the idea and, in 1891, it was introduced into City Council with the support of Mayor Edwin Stuart (1891–95). City Council referred the matter to James H. Windrim, director of public works, who prepared the first plan in 1892 illustrating a narrow parkway on axis with City Hall tower and Faire Mount. It was placed on the city map, then quickly removed in 1894 for lack of funding and so as not to create confusion for property owners.

Although the idea of a parkway preceded the 1893 Columbian World's Exposition, the exposition strongly influenced the eventual form the parkway was to take. Visitors to the exposition saw gleaming white buildings designed in a classical style connected by broad walkways and plazas. "The White City" stood in startling contrast to the gray and crowded character of most American cities after the Industrial Revolution. Philadelphia was no exception. As one of the leading manufacturing centers in the world at the end of the 19th century, manufacturing plants and smokestacks dominated the landscape throughout a greatly enlarged city with a population of 1.3 million.

The exposition drew the attention of architects and civic leaders to the European model on which it was based: the diagonal boulevards of Paris, created in the mid-19th century by Baron Haussmann, cutting through the chaos of Paris and linking new civic monuments and cultural institutions designed in a classical manner. Many cities quickly responded. In 1902, the McMillan Commission proposed a plan for Washington, D.C., based upon a pattern of diagonals; in Chicago, the Commercial Club, a civic association, commissioned Daniel Burnham, one of the planners of the exposition, to produce a new plan for that city. Burnham's 1909 plan was characterized by a series of diagonal boulevards.

Parkway Plan
1903
Albert Kelsey

In Philadelphia, the influence of the exposition led Albert Kelsey to revive the parkway idea and to become its champion. He organized civic support for the project, which led to the creation of the Parkway Association in 1902, the first in a series of civic organizations that would take leadership in promoting the parkway idea. Its members included the leading businessmen of the city: the president of the Baldwin Locomotive Company, the president of the Pennsylvania Railroad, streetcar magnate and developer Peter A. B. Widener and others. With their support, a new plan prepared by Albert Kelsey for a direct connection between City Hall and Faire Mount was put back on the city map in 1903.

The Parkway Association solicited the aid of two older and more established civic organizations—the Fairmount Park Art Association and the City Parks Association. With their support, municipal funds were appropriated and demolition of properties west of Logan Square began in 1907, although along a skewed path slightly different from Kelsey's plan to avoid certain costly real estate. There was little opposition to the proposed demolition of property. This section of the city was isolated by what was called the "Chinese Wall"—the elevated tracks of the Pennsylvania Railroad extending from 15th Street to 30th Street. But just as demolition was beginning in 1907, the plan for the parkway advanced significantly with

Parkway Plan

1907

Paul Philippe Cret,
Horace Trumbauer, and
Zantzinger and Borie

the election of Mayor John E. Reyburn (1907–11) and the intervention of Peter A. B. Widener.

Widener was one of the wealthiest men in the city and owner of an extraordinary art collection. His control over street railway lines allowed him to link transportation to land he owned creating what were referred to as "streetcar suburbs." For many years he had advocated for a new art museum to replace the inconveniently located one in Memorial Hall in Fairmount Park, implying that the donation of his art collection would follow. By 1907 the reservoir on top of Faire Mount no longer met the city's water supply needs. Widener saw this as the ideal location for a new museum and proposed the idea to newly elected Mayor Reyburn. Reyburn become a strong proponent of the plan and supported the idea of straightening the route of the parkway to make the Art Museum its terminus at one end and City Hall tower at the other.

Given this new opportunity, the Fairmount Park Art Association commissioned a comprehensive plan for the parkway. Paul Philippe Cret, a French-trained architect who had recently joined the architecture faculty at the University of Pennsylvania, C. Clark Zantzinger and his partner Charles L. Borie Jr., and Horace Trumbauer (Widener's favorite architect) were chosen to create the plan. Their 1907 plan changed not only the alignment, but also the basic

Parkway Plan
1915
Jacques Greber

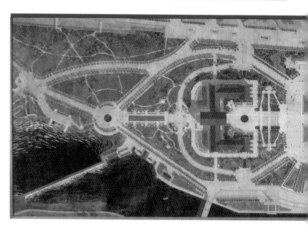

concept of the parkway. As Zantzinger stated: it is "not an extension of Fairmount Park which is being created. It is an avenue in the city giving access to Fairmount Park." This subtle change in vision was reflected in a plan that showed the parkway west of Logan Square lined with civic and cultural buildings, terminating in a grand plaza before the proposed art museum. Included in the plan were sites for two new art schools, a new Franklin Institute and a new Free Library. The plan also proposed narrowing the parkway between Logan Square and City Hall and creation of a grand plaza surrounded by civic buildings as a terminus for the parkway adjacent to City Hall.

This revised plan was placed on the city map in 1909. A model of the parkway was exhibited in City Hall at the First Municipal Planning Exhibition in America held in conjunction with the Third Annual City Planning Conference in 1911. Demolition proceeded and was essentially complete by 1915. Over 1,300 properties were demolished at a total cost of $35 million, a staggering sum at the time.

However, the story didn't end there. When the state legislature passed an act enabling cities to control all land within 200 feet of parkland, the city added the parkway to Fairmount Park. The Fairmount Park Commission adopted a set of design controls for everything within 200 feet of the parkway in 1916, effectively creating the city's first zoning plan. The controls, still in effect today, limit building heights and establish setbacks designed to maintain the narrow connection east of Logan Square in contrast to the broad and more open areas to the west. At the same time the Park Commission felt it appropriate to review the plans for the location of buildings and the landscape character. It hired Jacques Greber, a French landscape architect and planner. Greber worked on the parkway plans from 1917 to 1922 and defined the character it has today. He replanned the areas adjacent to the parkway, creating large open spaces and eliminating most of the cultural institutions shown in the 1907 Cret plan. In exchange he

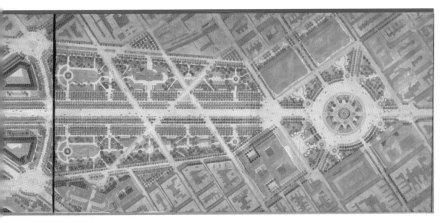

converted Logan Square to Logan Circle and modeled it after the Place de La Concorde in Paris. Here he placed the new Franklin Institute, Free Library, Municipal Court building and other institutions that had been previously distributed along the parkway or near City Hall. The plans developed by Greber—although modified when the parkway came to serve as a transportation artery—and the controls established in 1916 by the Fairmount Park Commission have guided the development of the parkway ever since.

The creation of the parkway was made possible by its connection with the new Art Museum. Initial plans for the museum were prepared separately by

Logan Circle, Free Library and Art Museum

c. 1930

Trumbauer and by Zantzinger and Borie. Julian Abele, Trumbauer's chief designer, returned from Greece with the idea of building three temples on a solid rock base. However, the final design appears to have been a compromise among all their ideas worked out by Howell Lewis Shay, an architect in Trumbauer's office. So difficult was fundraising for the project, that Eli Kirk Price, Park Commission member in charge of the project, ordered the two wings to be built first, knowing that Philadelphians wouldn't tolerate a gap in the middle. Begun in 1916, the museum finally opened in 1928.

The creation of the parkway, named after Benjamin Franklin in 1937, is one of the great city planning accomplishments in Philadelphia's history. The effort to create the parkway generated the first direct participation in city planning by civic leaders and led to the first real interest in planning on the part of the city government. The formation of the Parkway Association—an organization of business and civic leaders that promoted the parkway idea—established a precedent for a form of civic leadership in city planning that became characteristic of Philadelphia throughout the 20th century.

THE DECADE OF BIG IDEAS
1920–1930

Developed area in 1925

For Mayor John Reyburn the Parkway and the Art Museum were just the beginning of a transformation of "a great city into a greater city." Reyburn was a man of broad vision. He had served 16 years in the U.S. Congress before returning to Philadelphia as mayor. He embraced the new vision of Philadelphia—represented by the Parkway and advocated by Kelsey, Crawford and others—of a city linked together by diagonal roads. To extend the concepts of the City Beautiful movement throughout the city he appointed a Committee on Comprehensive Plans in 1909.

Joseph Widener, son and heir of Peter A. B. Widener, chaired the committee, which was composed of prominent civic leaders. Reyburn organized subcommittees on a variety of different topics, thereby bringing together an even larger group of business, civic, and community leaders. The first report of the Committee, delivered to Mayor Reyburn in 1911, presented detailed recommendations on a broad range of issues, including:

- completion of the Parkway;
- development of a new convention hall in Fairmount Park with an auditorium suitable for concerts and an adjacent municipal sports stadium;
- preservation of land adjacent to city creeks as open space and parkland; and
- improvement of piers along the waterfront.

City Hall Plaza
1911
John T. Windrim

The report also proposed that the Committee be made permanent and continue to work with the city on plans for the future. Reyburn endorsed the recommendations and immediately sought funds for completing the Parkway. With City Council approval the Committee was made permanent in 1912, and new Mayor Rudolph Blankenberg (1911–16) appointed what was in effect Philadelphia's first city planning commission.

The Committee's 1915 report suggested additional projects of importance to the city. These included:

- creation of a "traffic loop" around the primary commercial center of the city by widening Race Street, Locust Street, 16th Street, and 8th Street;
- development of a comprehensive code limiting

heights of buildings and dividing the city into three land-use zones; and

• free public lectures on city planning and programs for children in the city schools, with textbooks and films about city planning.

By 1919 the value of city planning had been sufficiently accepted by both civic and political leadership that the creation of a City Planning Commission as well as a Zoning Commission was included in the new City Charter. While the Zoning Commission was appointed quickly, Republican mayors saw public works projects primarily as opportunities for patronage jobs and had little interest in planning. It would be 10 years before any members were appointed to the City Planning Commission and 23 years before professional planners were hired to staff it.

Notwithstanding the absence of a planning commission, the decade of the 1920s was an extraordinary decade for planning and development in Philadelphia. Fueled by an influx of immigrants, the population of the city grew to nearly two million. This necessitated planning for such transportation projects as the Delaware River Bridge and expansion of the subway system. By 1930, a wide range of planning ideas had been proposed and Center City witnessed a construction explosion that produced many of its most notable high-rise buildings.

**Constitution Square
north of
Independence Hall**
1923

City Council President Charles Hall started things off in 1923 by proposing the construction of a 17-story municipal office building at Juniper and Filbert streets. He also endorsed the proposal of Mrs. E. T. Stotesbury, wife of prominent banker Edward T. Stotesbury, to demolish the area from 5th and 6th streets from Chestnut to Market streets to create a park that would be an appropriate setting for Independence Hall. In 1924, newly elected Mayor W. Freeland Kendrick (1924–28) announced an ambitious development agenda. So extensive were the ideas proposed in that year that Andrew Wright Crawford, secretary of the City Parks Association, stated: "Ten years hence 1924 will be regarded as having been the dawn of a great expansion in Philadelphia." In many respects, Crawford was right. During Kendrick's term, most of the planning ideas that would transform Philadelphia in the 1950s were first proposed. Among them were:

- a new railroad station at 30th Street with a new Post Office adjacent to it;

- an Episcopal Cathedral on Logan Square;

- a new convention hall next to the Art Museum;

- a new municipal stadium in South Philadelphia;

- demolition of the Broad Street Station of the Pennsylvania Railroad and construction of a new underground rail station at 16th and Market streets;

- widening of Filbert Street west of City Hall to the Schuylkill River and renaming it Pennsylvania Boulevard;

- improving the west bank of the Schuylkill River from Spring Garden Street to South Street in conjunction with the construction of the new train station at 30th Street; and

- straightening the Market Street subway under City Hall and creating a lower level pedestrian concourse from 13th to 15th streets and Locust to Race streets.

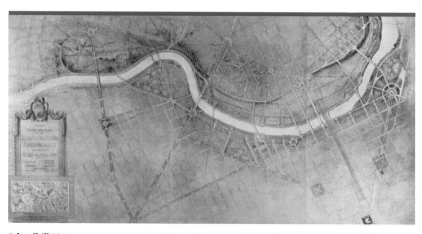

Schuylkill River waterfront plan
1924
Paul Philippe Cret

Plans for the proposed improvement of the Schuylkill River waterfront were developed by Paul Philippe Cret for the Philadelphia Commission, a civic organization headed by the president of the Pennsylvania Railroad. They included plans for a Sesquicentennial Exposition in 1926. At the same time Cret also advanced the startling idea that City Hall should be demolished, with the exception of the tower, and a complex of new municipal and civic buildings built in the surrounding area.

Although the Pennsylvania Railroad agreed to demolish the Broad Street Station, it indicated that it would not do so until three years after the completion of the new station at 30th Street. The new station was not completed until 1934, which would have meant demolition should have taken place in 1937, but the Depression and the country's entry into World War II delayed demolition until 1952. How-

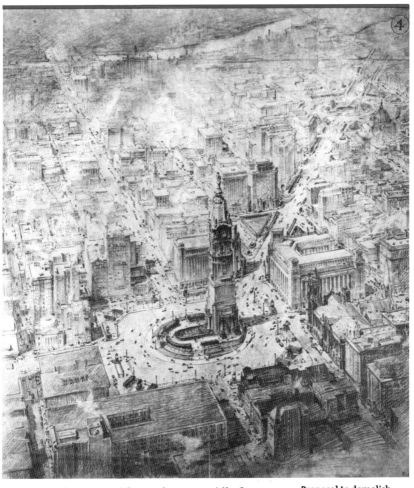

Proposal to demolish City Hall

1924

Paul Philippe Cret

ever, other plans moved forward more rapidly. In 1927, the widening of Filbert Street to the Schuylkill River began and was heralded by the *Philadelphia Bulletin* as the "opening of the second canto of the Epic of Transformation of Philadelphia" of which the development of the Parkway had been the first. Most spectacular of all was the number of skyscrapers erected in Center City in 1929–30: the Lewis Tower, the Drake, the Rittenhouse Plaza, the Chateau Crillon, the Suburban Station office building, the Sun Oil Company office building, the Market Street National Bank, the 22-story Penn Mutual Life Insurance Co. addition, the Architects Building, the 30-story addition to the Girard Trust and the PSFS Building —the first American skyscraper designed in the International style. Not until the 1950s would Philadelphia experience an equivalent building boom.

Perhaps it was this extraordinary magnitude of development that finally convinced the city government that a planning commission was needed, for in 1929, Mayor Harry Mackey (1928–32), influenced by civic leadership, finally appointed members to the commission. Mayor Mackey was particularly concerned with the condition of the city east of Broad Street. As residential development had moved steadily westward toward Rittenhouse Square and new residential areas for the growing middle class were developed in North and West Philadelphia, the older sections of Center City were overwhelmed by a continuing influx of immigrants. Mackey turned to the Committee on Child Welfare and Recreation, chaired by philanthropist Samuel Fleischer, to look into the overcrowded housing conditions and come up with a plan to make the area "a beautiful and comfortable residential section for the plain people." The Committee's plan, created with the assistance of the Philadelphia Housing Association, covered the area from Broad Street to the Delaware River, Poplar to Carpenter streets. It recommended the preservation of the historic shrines (Independence Hall and related buildings and historic churches) with the demolition of slum housing conditions to be replaced by new two-story dwellings in a manner that would provide more light and air.

However, these concerns did not take center stage in 1930 when the newly appointed planning commission produced what it referred to as a 50-year plan for Philadelphia. To develop this ambitious plan, the commission had turned to Jacques Greber, planner of the Parkway, for assistance. Greber helped produce a plan with a vast array of projects, incorporating many earlier ideas while also proposing new ones. Among the ideas in this plan were:

- new approaches to the recently completed Delaware River Bridge;
- further development of the Parkway, including completion of Logan Square and the civic buildings intended to surround it;
- single- and double-decked roadways on the east and west banks of the Schuylkill River;
- a new building on Reyburn Plaza adjacent to City Hall;
- a court of honor from Market to Chestnut streets to provide a better setting for Independence Hall (Mayor S. Davis Wilson extended this idea in 1936 into a plan covering the area from Chestnut to Vine streets that included places for all the states of the union along with modern apartment houses, office buildings, theaters and attractive parks.);
- the demolition of the Broad Street Station and construction of an office complex above the tracks extending from 15th to 30th streets;
- extension of the Locust Street subway from 18th Street under the river and on through West Philadelphia; and

Development over railroad tracks, 15th Street to Schuylkill River

1939

• several major road improvements to create diagonal arteries from one end of the city to another, including an elevated roadway paralleling the Delaware River.

Although Philadelphia architects, led by Milton Medary, president of the local chapter of the American Institute of Architects, continued to press for the demolition of City Hall, the Planning Commission rejected the idea. If it was not possible to create a complete composition of classical buildings in the surrounding area, they stated, it was best to leave City Hall as it was.

Not only were ambitious plans put forth for the city, but in 1924 the Regional Planning Federation was formed to consider the future growth and development of the Philadelphia region. In 1932, it issued a 10-volume, 500-page plan for the Tri State Philadelphia District. This was the only significant regional planning activity until Penjerdel was formed in 1957 to conduct regional research, followed by creation of the Delaware Valley Regional Planning Commission in 1965.

The Depression put a sudden halt to all these ambitious plans. Mayor J. Hampton Moore (1932–36) put it simply when he said there was no money. However, Moore's successor, Mayor S. Davis Wilson (1936–39), took advantage of funding from the federal Works Progress Administration to support construction of many projects, including the Municipal Court building on Logan Square. The WPA also funded the first land-use survey of every property in the city, which provided the basis for Philadelphia's first zoning code, adopted in 1933. (No other comprehensive land-use survey would be done for over 30 years.) It also surveyed the city's historic resources and produced a detailed guidebook of the city in 1937.

As city historian Margaret B. Tinkcom would later note of this period from 1920 to 1930: "Although much that was then proposed or partially executed died on the drawing boards, silent victims of the Depression, the plans and unfinished public works of the Mackey era were ready at hand when a new Planning Commission and reform government took charge of the city twenty years later."

THE BACON ERA
1940–1980

Developed area in 1950

Although the planning accomplishments of the period from 1940 to 1970 were the result of the actions of many people, Edmund N. Bacon was the central figure in the development of plans that provided direction for the city. Bacon was trained as an architect at Cornell and worked in Flint, Michigan, on traffic and housing studies sponsored by the WPA. He was brought back to Philadelphia by his friend Walter Phillips, an attorney with an interest in political reform. Phillips organized a new civic group, the City Policy Committee, and, with Bacon's assistance, pushed for the creation of a professionally staffed municipal planning commission. Although Republican Mayor Bernard Samuels (1941–52) had no interest in planning, the support of Edward Hopkinson Jr., one of the city's most prominent businessmen, led to the passage of a City Council ordinance establishing such a commission in 1942. Robert Mitchell was hired as its first executive director. Mitchell felt the Planning Commission should focus on research and capital projects that could be completed quickly to build public confidence in planning. As his first task he assembled all of the planning ideas of the 1920s and 1930s into a reference volume—referred to as "the bible"—that guided the staff's work.

Mitchell and his staff set out to produce a capital program for the city, drawing on the numerous plans previously proposed and on a list of needed projects solicited from all public agencies. The document, released in 1945, listed over 1,000 projects in all sections of the city to be completed by 1950. Of these, 600 were noted as high priority, with a total cost of $200 million. This was not a "plan," something Mitchell deliberately avoided; it was a catalogue of the many capital improvements the city needed after enduring the Depression and diversion of resources necessary to support the war effort. Among the projects listed were most of the proposals that had been made for Center City in the 1920s including demolition of the Broad Street Station, along with development over the railroad tracks out to 30th Street Station, and the creation of a court of honor in front of Independence Hall. In addition, there were proposals for projects needed to improve and maintain the infrastructure of sewage collection and treatment, water purification, roadways, schools and health-care facilities. The report was truly comprehensive, both in its geographic scope and in the range of needs it addressed.

To support the work of the City Planning Commission, the Citizens Council on City Planning was founded in 1943. It sponsored studies by architects Oskar Stonorov and Louis I. Kahn for the re-planning of residential neighborhoods. This work encouraged Stonorov and Kahn to conceive the idea for an exhibition about planning for Philadelphia. Stonorov enlisted his friend Edmund Bacon in the project. Bacon was then serving in the Navy, but began working on the idea; when he returned in 1945 all three worked in earnest to organize the exhibit, with Robert Mitchell's support. The Better Philadelphia Exhibition opened in Gimbel's Department store in Center City in 1947. Over 385,000 visitors came to see exhibits, plans and models of what Philadelphia might look like in 25 years. One display included a map with lights showing the location of every one of the projects in the Planning Commission's $200 million capital program. The central feature of the exhibit was a huge model of Center City, sections of which flipped over to show first what that part of Center City looked like in 1947 and what it might look like in 1982. All of the future ideas were invented by Stonorov, Kahn and Bacon. The exhibition inspired both the residents of Philadelphia and those who sought political reform to value city planning as an important activity.

Within a remarkably short period of time, the ingredients for change fell into place. Congress passed the first Housing Act in 1949; a second Housing Act in 1954 provided the broader powers and funding that would enable American cities to plan and undertake the major urban renewal projects long contemplated in Philadelphia. In 1945, the Pennsylvania legislature passed authorization for redevelopment authorities with the power to condemn land. Philadelphia was one of the first cities in the nation to create such an agency. From 1947 to 1955, planning emphasized complete demolition of those neighborhoods in the city in the worst condition, most of them outside of Center City, followed by new development. The city's first redevelopment project of this type was the Yorktown residential community in North Philadelphia, dating from 1948. Other urban renewal projects were identified in North Philadelphia and the development of Eastwick, in the southwest section of the city, was proposed to provide a new community for "negroes" displaced by other projects.

Better Philadelphia Exhibit, model of Center City

1947

Oskar Stonorov, Louis I. Kahn, Edmund N. Bacon, Robert Mitchell

Public dissatisfaction with the corruption of Mayor Samuel's administration resulted in electoral approval of a new City Charter in 1951 that gave stronger powers to the mayor and redefined the role of the Planning Commission by requiring it to produce a comprehensive plan for the city, as well as a six-year capital budget. Neither Mitchell nor Bacon, who became executive director of the Planning Commission in 1949, had any interest in comprehensive planning. It wasn't until 1957 that a comprehensive planning division was created as a result of pressure from civic groups and from William Rafsky, executive director of the Redevelopment Authority. The city's first comprehensive plan was published in 1960.

The approval of a new charter was accompanied by the election of Joseph S. Clark, Jr. (1952–56), the first Democratic mayor of the century, to be followed in 1956 by the election of Democrat Richardson Dilworth (1956–62). Clark and Dilworth cleaned house, professionalized the city government and placed the revitalization of Center City at the top of their political agendas. In 1954, Mayor Clark's administration produced the first systematic planning proposal for the renewal of Philadelphia. It was prepared by the Redevelopment Authority rather than the Planning Commission and indicated the differences in both planning approach and renewal strategy between Edmund Bacon of the Planning Commission and William Rafsky and David Wallace, executive director and chief of planning, respectively, of the Authority. The CURA Report, as it was known, contained alternative renewal policies for the city, carefully documenting the cost of implementation of each. While there was agreement among both the Planning Commission and Redevelopment Authority that Center City had to be a key focus of any planning, there were distinct differences of opinion about a larger strategy. Rafsky and Wallace favored abandoning the large-scale slum clearance approach in favor of a strategy focusing on investing in neighborhoods that were declining but still viable. Bacon preferred to continue large-scale clearance projects, an approach that prevailed, in part due to the guidelines of federal funding.

Mayor Dilworth made the renewal of Center City his highest priority. As a symbol of his commitment to the revitalization of the eastern part of the city, which was considered a slum, Dilworth and his wife built a house for themselves on Washington Square. Dilworth was also instrumental in reviving the type of civic/political partnership that had been successful in the development and implementation of planning projects earlier in the century. At his invitation, leaders of the business community created the Old Philadelphia Development Corporation (OPDC)

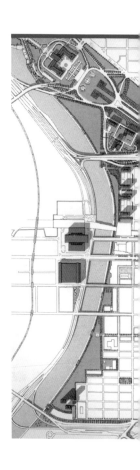

in 1956 to partner with the city in the implementation of planning projects. OPDC would first take responsibility for assisting with the redevelopment of Society Hill. Over time it would bring together civic and business leaders to support each of the many Center City projects initiated by city government, and then go on to create several of its own.

By the end of the 1950s, a system of planning and implementation was in place. The City Planning Commission produced preliminary plans for redevelopment areas, which were converted to urban renewal plans by the Redevelopment Authority, which received funding for project implementation from the federal urban renewal program. OPDC was in place to bring the support of the business community to bear on marketing and sale of property. Key to the initial success of this venture was William Rafsky. In various roles from housing coordinator, to executive director of the Redevelopment Authority, executive director of OPDC and development coordinator to the mayor, Rafsky held together the network of agencies and provided the management leadership that would result in a coordinated implementation of ambitious plans.

The 1963 Center City Plan provided the framework for these efforts. By the time it was published many of its major proposals were already well under way. However, the plan provides a good understand-

Center City Plan
1963
Philadelphia City Planning
Commission

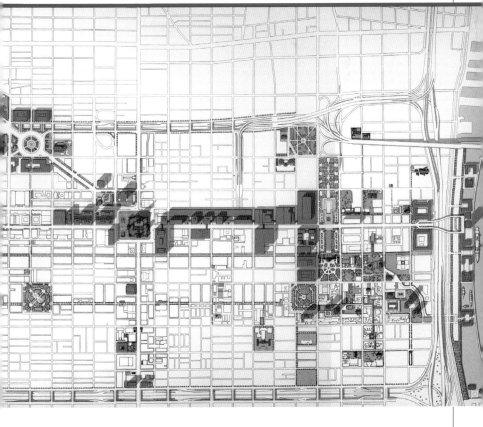

ing of the vision for Center City that developed in
the 1950s under Bacon's direction. Although the plan
included many projects previously proposed in the
1920s, it brought those projects together and added
others to create a unified vision for Center City ad-
dressing each of its critical components. Bacon's illus-
tration of planning proposals in architectural terms
and his effectiveness as a public speaker inspired business leaders and the public to believe that these plans
were both desirable and feasible.

The major components of this vision presented
in the 1963 Plan were:

- an expressway loop surrounding Center City on
  all four sides, with direct connections to parking
  garages;

- a water-related museum and recreation area
  along the Delaware River;

- a public park along the Schuylkill River from
  the Art Museum to South Street;

- rehabilitation of the older residential area renamed Society Hill into an affluent residential
  neighborhood;

- a national park surrounding Independence Hall;

- a mall and office area north of Independence
  Hall;

- a new retail shopping project linking major
  department stores, supported by a new underground railroad station replacing the Reading
  Terminal at 12th Street;

- conversion of Chestnut Street to a pedestrian
  shopping mall;

- a new office complex on the site of a demolished
  Broad Street Station; and

- a performing arts district along South Broad
  Street.

The plan was widely publicized in professional
magazines and led to Bacon being featured on the
cover of *Time* Magazine in 1964.

Although projects were worked on simultane-
ously, their implementation followed approximately
this sequence:

Penn Center: In 1952, the Pennsylvania Railroad
began demolition of the Broad Street Station as had
been agreed in the 1920s. When it announced plans
for the proposed office complex that would replace
the station, Bacon, with the assistance of architect
Vincent G. Kling, offered an alternative plan. Their
plan suggested an open-air pedestrian shopping
promenade at the same lower level as Suburban Station. In the end, the railroad incorporated a few gardens and entrances to the lower level into its plan, but
not of sufficient magnitude to enable the concourse

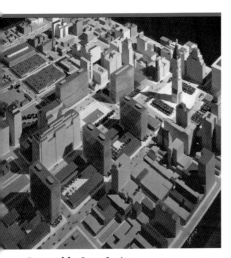

Proposal for Penn Center
1952
Edmund Bacon and
Vincent G. Kling

to take on the character Bacon and Kling had envisioned. The office buildings constructed in 1953—modest and architecturally undistinguished—were the first in Center City since the great building boom of 1929.

Coupled with Penn Center was the redevelopment of the public areas around City Hall. A new plaza was created to the west, a new municipal office building built on Reyburn Plaza similar to that proposed by Greber in 1930, and an underground parking garage and plaza built in the block terminating the Parkway. Bacon joined the ranks of earlier architects and planners by calling for the demolition of all but the tower of City Hall. However, the idea was abandoned when engineers determined the cost of demolishing the building's 22-foot-thick masonry walls. Today it is one of Center City's most admired buildings.

Independence National Historical Park: Independence National Historical Park, first proposed in 1948, was authorized in 1956. The National Park Service began the restoration of Independence Hall and other key historic buildings. It also acquired and demolished surrounding buildings to create a parklike setting for the historic properties.

**Independence Mall
and East Mall**
1944
Roy F. Larson

Independence Mall: Another civic organization, the Independence Mall Association headed by Judge Edwin O. Lewis, revived the plan created in 1944 for a mall in front of Independence Hall. The Commonwealth of Pennsylvania condemned the three blocks of property in front of Independence Hall in 1953 and the Redevelopment Authority augmented this by condemning property to the east and west to create an office center. Although land was cleared by 1960, it took until 1965 to complete all three blocks of the mall. The Rohm and Haas Company placed its new headquarters building on 6th Street in 1960, but the market for private office buildings was limited. Public buildings took their place: a new U.S. Mint, Federal Office Building and the Federal Reserve Bank.

Society Hill: Plans for the renewal of the Society Hill area were begun in 1956. The entire area was surveyed to identify buildings of the colonial and federal era to be saved and all others were marked for demolition. The plan was described as the first to use historic preservation as the basis for community revitalization. But historic preservation was not very developed in the 1950s. The plans for Society Hill—as well as the plans for the National Park and Independence Mall—focused on preserving only those historic buildings of the 18th and early-19th centuries. Hundreds of later 19th-century buildings were demolished, including numerous 19th-century cast iron commercial buildings and many distinctive bank buildings designed by Frank Furness. However, the interest in historic properties prompted by the renewal of Society Hill resulted in the creation of the Philadelphia Historical Commission in 1955. The Commission began surveying and designating historic properties immediately, but it would take over two decades before preservation became a part of city planning in Philadelphia.

In Society Hill, the Old Philadelphia Development Corporation (OPDC) sold all of the colonial houses to private individuals who would rehabilitate them. On vacant lots contemporary new construction was encouraged. A system of pedestrian greenways was introduced that further encouraged investment in the area. The great symbol of transformation was a new residential project made possible by the earlier decision to relocate the Dock Street markets to a new food distribution center in South Philadelphia. The competition winning design by I. M. Pei for three modern apartment towers became a landmark on the city skyline, symbolizing the transformation of the neighborhood. Although it would take until 1980 to complete the sale of land acquired in the urban renewal program, Society Hill quickly became a success. Rather than a place for the "plain people" as Mayor Mackey had once proposed, it attracted wealthy civic and business leaders to return to the city, as well as young families eager to be urban pioneers.

Society Hill houses during restoration
1956

Market Street East: Plans for revitalization of the retail shopping area began in the 1950s as well, including a proposal to create a tunnel linking the Pennsylvania Railroad's underground railroad station at 16th Street with a new underground station at 11th Street to replace the Reading Terminal. However, it wasn't until 1964 that a plan won the support of OPDC's Market East Committee of prominent businessmen. This plan proposed a lower level concourse, similar to Bacon's Penn Center concept, with a dramatic, skylit multi-level shopping mall. The plan was featured in a special story on planning in Philadelphia in *Life* Magazine in 1965. The first phase of what became known as The Gallery at Market East, one of the nation's first inner city shopping malls, was completed by the Rouse Company, a prominent

Market East Plan
1964
Philadelphia City Planning Commission

developer of suburban shopping malls, in 1977. A
second phase was completed in 1984.

The plan for Market East is another indication
of the limited concern for historic preservation during this period. The plan proposed the demolition of
the historic Reading Terminal train shed and head
house office building. Both buildings were saved, not
because of a change of attitude by the planners but
because—as with City Hall—money was not available to undertake their demolition. They were
preserved in the 1990s as part of the Pennsylvania
Convention Center.

Other Plans: Plans for other projects included in the
1963 Center City Plan proceeded more slowly. Penn's
Landing, the new waterfront project on the Delaware
River, did not begin until the late 1970s. A public

**Penn's Landing on
the Delaware River
waterfront**

plaza and museum were built, but development was hampered because I-95 separated the site from the city. Over the
years, many plans would be proposed for
Penn's Landing, but by 2007 none have
come to fruition.

Expressways: The first expression of
public dissatisfaction with the recommendations of the 1963 Center City
Plan focused on the proposals for expressways. The plan incorporated the
plans for the creation of Interstate 95
along the Delaware River. The expressway was elevated and ran parallel to the river from the southwest to northeast sections of Philadelphia, similar to
that proposed in Greber's plans in 1930. However,
new residents in Society Hill expressed opposition to
the elevated expressway cutting off their connection
to the river. In spite of support by the City Planning
Commission and OPDC, in 1971 the citizens committee opposing the project was successful in getting the
Center City section of the expressway depressed and
covered, thereby maintaining some connection to the
riverfront.

The proposed expressway on the south side of
Center City was also opposed by neighborhood organizations that did not want to see the vital commercial area along South Street demolished or to see
further displacement of African American residents.
Concerned Citizens for the Crosstown Expressway,
with the assistance of urban planner Denise Scott
Brown, was successful in having the expressway
dropped from the city plans in 1971, notwithstanding
support for it by the Planning Commission and
OPDC.

What might be considered the last significant
planning effort of this era occurred at the end of the
1960s when Philadelphia began to look ahead to the

200th anniversary of the founding of the nation in 1976. A committee of civic leaders had been appointed to develop ideas for the Bicentennial. They were challenged by a group of younger, emerging civic leaders who felt the city should seek to host an international exposition of the character that had been held in Montreal, Canada, in 1967. This group promoted the idea of development over the railroad tracks north of 30th Street Station, a site that had emerged in many people's minds as the next place for major urban development. The idea gained public support and was eventually adopted. The Bicentennial Corporation hired urban planner David A. Crane, under whose auspices the concept for the Bicentennial was broadened to include not only the development of the 30th Street area, but also a citywide agenda of urban improvement projects. Lack of support from the Nixon Administration eventually put an end to the idea of an international exposition and Philadelphia settled for a more modest historic celebration.

30th Street Station area circulation plan

1970

Mitchell/Giurgola Associates

However, the Bicentennial encouraged Philadelphia and the nation to look at its historic assets. The passage of the Tax Reform Act of 1976 provided investment tax credits for rehabilitation of historic properties. To demonstrate the potential of the new tax credits for community renewal, a plan was created for Old City and the area designated a National Register Historic District in 1980. This led to the rehabilitation of many former commercial buildings and the creation of hundreds of units of housing. To further historic preservation, OPDC established the Philadelphia Historic Preservation Corporation, a separate non-profit organization devoted solely to historic preservation, and predecessor to today's Preservation Alliance for Greater Philadelphia. Henceforth, historic preservation became a component of Center City planning and community revitalization.

Although planning in this period placed a primary emphasis on physical design and architectural images, behind the scenes many other important city planning activities were accomplished. A subdivision code was adopted in 1952 giving the Planning Commission the ability to implement plans Bacon had initiated in 1949 for the development of the Far Northeast section of the city. The comprehensive plan adopted in 1960 was consistently supported by a six-year capital budget prepared by the Planning Commission and updated annually. The Zoning Code adopted in 1933 was revised in 1962 and in 1965 a new property inventory of the city was begun.

While these accomplishments were the work of many people, the period of Edmund Bacon's tenure as executive director was the "golden era" of city planning in Philadelphia. When Bacon retired in 1970, most of the plans proposed in the 1963 Plan were well under way or had sufficient support that they continued to be the focus of public and private efforts through the rest of the century.

In spite of the progress with implementation of projects in the 1963 Plan, by 1968 the context of planning in Philadelphia had begun to change. Opposition to I-95 and the Crosstown Expressway were among the first signs of a growing dissatisfaction with the large-scale demolition of the urban renewal era, the failure to include residents in the planning process and a failure to give as much attention to Philadelphia's neighborhoods as to Center City. In 1968, the federal government, responding to similar concerns at a national level, established the Model Cities Program and shifted funding to a greater focus on programs to address urban poverty. In 1972, President Nixon ended all funding for urban renewal activities. The 1974 Housing Act created Community Development Block Grants (CDBG) to allow cities greater flexibility on how to invest in urban revitalization. But federal guidelines for the use of CDBG funds increasingly emphasized a focus on housing and neighborhood revitalization instead of large downtown projects. While the Urban Development Action Grant (UDAG) program of the Carter administration would lend some support to Center City development projects, the federal focus remained on neighborhood revitalization.

Philadelphia responded to these shifts by creating a complicated community participation structure for implementation of the Model Cities program, involving leadership from the black community in a significant way for the first time. Later, in 1976, Mayor Frank Rizzo (1972–80) created the Office of Housing and Community Development (OHCD), responding to criticisms that the city was not using its CDBG funds effectively to revitalize neighborhoods. Although the City Planning Commission provided some initial direction on potential neighborhood revitalization areas, after 1976 most development decisions were made by OHCD. A neighborhood focus, with relatively little planning behind it, would remain a priority of city government into the first years of the 21st century.

ECONOMIC DEVELOPMENT TO THE FOREFRONT

1980–2006

Developed area in 1983

The impetus for renewed interest in Center City planning came in 1984 when developer Willard Rouse proposed an office building that would exceed the height of the City Hall tower. Throughout the 1950s and 1960s there had been a "gentlemen's agreement" that no buildings would exceed the height of the tower—491 feet to the base of the statue of William Penn at its top. Rouse's proposal sparked public interest and vociferous debate. Bacon emerged from retirement to oppose the plan, while others supported it. In the end City Council approved the proposed development and in 1987 the 960-foot-tall One Liberty Place office building was completed.

This debate about height led to a concern about the location of further tall buildings and encouraged the Planning Commission to begin work on a new Center City Plan in 1985. Published in 1988, the plan was radically different from the plan published in 1963. While the 1963 plan was brief—containing only 40 pages—and extensively illustrated with architectural drawings of future projects, the 175-page 1988 Plan consisted mainly of text and diagrams. The emphasis of this new plan was not a series of new projects, but strategies to achieve growth while protecting Center City neighborhoods. The plan was based on very optimistic projections for office development and residential population. To accommodate the projected office growth an

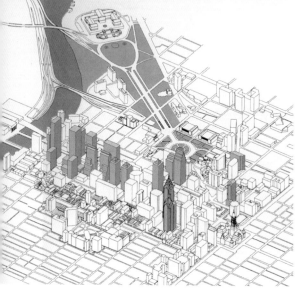

Center City Plan
1988
Philadelphia City
Planning Commission

area for new tall office buildings was designated, adjacent to and west of Penn Center. In subsequent years, three more office buildings taller than City Hall tower were completed in this area and in 2006 construction began on a fourth, which will be the tallest building in the city. New zoning controls were adopted to preserve light and air on key streets, and a system of zoning bonuses instituted to encourage public plazas and open space. "View corridors" were identified to protect the view of City Hall tower.

Plans for five districts recommended more specific development projects including a new convention center in the Reading Terminal train shed and a performing arts district along South Broad Street. One of the key recommendations of the plan was the creation of a downtown management entity, supported by a special tax assessment, to maintain streets, sidewalks and public places. However, the most important new policy to preserve neighborhood character was the revision of the city's historic preservation ordinance in 1985 to allow the designation of historic districts in addition to individual buildings. Subsequently, Society Hill, Old City and the Rittenhouse Square neighborhood all were designated as districts to protect their historic character.

However, the optimism inherent in the 1988 Plan did not last. It was dashed in 1990 when a national recession pushed Philadelphia into a new fiscal crisis that would affect the attitude of city government toward planning for years to come.

Although the projects identified in the 1963 Center City Plan continued to be the focus of attention, planning for Center City since 1990 has been shaped by steadily declining economic circumstances of the city as a whole. Philadelphia has consistently lost residents since 1950, when the population peaked at over two million. In 2005, according to the U.S. Census Bureau, Philadelphia's population stood at 1.4 million. From 1990 to 1996, Philadelphia ranked first in the nation in population decline.

Philadelphia has also lost jobs and Center City has experienced a steady drop in office employment and in its share of the region's office market. The downtown retail base also experienced lean years, with retail stores declining by 32% and Center City's share of regional sales dropping from 15% to 6% between 1954 and 1977.

A sense of urgency about the city's economic future led mayors from Frank L. Rizzo to John F. Street (2000–08) to place greater emphasis on economic development than on planning. The purpose of planning increasingly became one of not impeding private development in whatever form and in whatever location it might occur—an attitude that has prevailed up to the current moment.

In the 1990s, the concern for economic development focused on strengthening the city's hospitality and tourism industry through a series of projects initiated by government and by civic organizations. The 1988 Center City Plan highlighted the importance of constructing a new convention center. With assistance from the state, the Pennsylvania Convention Center was com-

Pennsylvania Convention Center Grand Hall
1994

pleted, preserving the historic Reading Terminal train shed as a distinctive feature. The city provided economic incentives to attract new hotels, many of which were created by converting historic office buildings.

A second element of the 1988 Plan was the creation of a performing arts district along South Broad Street, an idea first advanced in the 1960s. The Central Philadelphia Development Corporation (CPDC), the renamed Old Philadelphia Development Corporation established by the business community and Mayor Dilworth in 1956, took up this challenge, commissioning planning and economic studies in 1990 and 1992. At the same time, the Philadelphia Orchestra announced its intention to build a new orchestra hall. Much like the Parkway and Art Museum in the early part of the century, the merger of these two ideas strengthened them both. With Mayor Edward G. Rendell's (1992–2000) energetic support, $265 million was raised to build a new orchestra hall as part of the Kimmel Center for the Performing Arts, which became the centerpiece of the Avenue of the Arts district. Within a relatively short time, several new theaters were completed, new sidewalks and streetlights installed, and a high school for the performing arts created through the conversion of a vacant historic building.

A third component of this focus on tourism was the decision of the Independence National Historical Park to redesign Independence Mall and to create a center for the commemoration of the U.S. Constitution. While most people agreed that the public space of the mall might be better designed, the proposal to rebuild it fostered considerable public debate. Edmund Bacon came out of retirement once again to oppose the plans. However, in 1999 the Park Service

Avenue of the Arts plan
1992
Kise Franks Straw

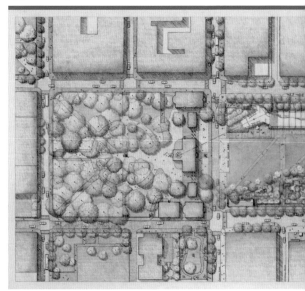

Logan Square improvement plan, Center City District

2006

Lager Raabe Skafte

adopted a plan that included construction of a new visitor center, a new building to house the Liberty Bell and the National Constitution Center.

CPDC further contributed to this focus on tourism by undertaking a reexamination of the Benjamin Franklin Parkway in 1999. The plan proposed a return to the ideas advanced by Paul Philippe Cret in 1907 for a parkway lined with more buildings and thus with more activity. These plans led to a series of public improvements, including the lighting of public buildings and public art along the Parkway as well as City Hall. The possibility of several new museums—including the controversial move of the Barnes Foundation school and art collection from Lower Merion to Center City—and the need for Art Museum expansion, have encouraged CPDC to undertake further planning studies for the Parkway.

As was true in other periods, government's declining interest in Center City planning was taken up by civic associations and nonprofit organizations. Key among these was CPDC. In addition to plans for the Avenue of the Arts and the Parkway, CPDC promptly responded to one of the principal recommendations of the 1988 Plan—the creation of a downtown management corporation. The Center City District (CCD) was created in 1990 to undertake maintenance and management of public places, with support from a special tax assessment. CCD quickly began to implement an ambitious program of sidewalk cleaning, marketing and promotion, provision of public signs, landscaping and other improvements.

Although CPDC and CCD were the lead civic organizations engaged in planning during this period, others undertook major initiatives as well. In 2002, the Schuylkill River Development Council led the effort to implement the Schuylkill River Park pro-

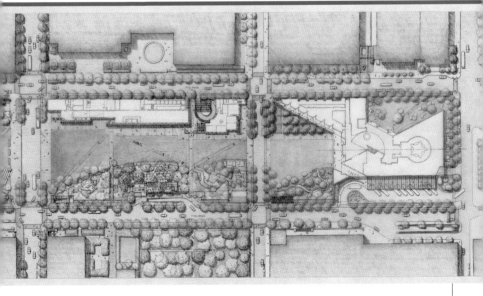

Independence Mall Master Plan

1999

Olin Partnership

45

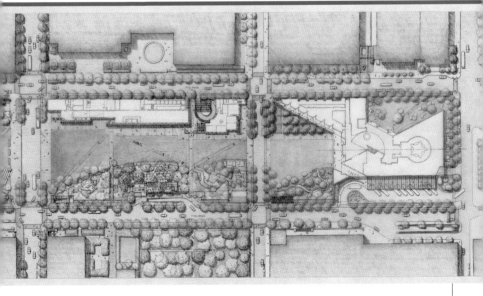

ECONOMIC DEVELOPMENT TO THE FOREFRONT

posed in the 1963 Plan and, in 2003, its Tidal
Schuylkill Plan established a comprehensive approach to the river that has been continued by the
Schuylkill River Development Corporation. Neighborhood organizations in Old City, Society Hill and
the Rittenhouse Square area planned for the future
of their neighborhoods by securing designation as
historic districts.

Support for new residential development was
provided in 1997 when City Council, at the initiative
of Councilman Frank DiCicco, approved a 10-year tax
abatement for conversion of vacant or under-utilized
office buildings to residential use. In the period from
its adoption to 2005, over 8,200 new residential units
were created, mainly through the adaptive re-use of
historic properties. Although the city as a whole continued to lose population, Center City began to gain
residents, leading, to many new restaurants and revival of some retail areas. The success of the tax
abatement program led City Council in 2000 to provide a similar incentive for new residential construction prompting rapid condominium development.
The desire to take fullest advantage of this housing
boom in the period from 2004 on led to an attitude of
almost *laissez-faire* development of the part of public
agencies. Zoning variances well beyond anything contemplated by the 1988 Plan became routine, much to
the dismay of civic and neighborhood organizations.
While contributing to the further growth of housing
and Center City population, the impact of new high-
rise residential proposals on neighborhood character
has become one of the major planning controversies
of recent years.

In the absence of planning by city government,
neighborhood organizations sought their own protec-
tion: Old City secured a 65-foot height limit for new
construction (only to have the law ignored by the
Zoning Board at the end of 2006); the Rittenhouse
Square neighborhood produced its own plan in 2007;
and City Council passed a height limit restriction for
neighborhoods west of Broad Street in the face of
several controversial proposals for residential towers—including one for development over the railroad
tracks east of 30th Street Station first proposed in the
1920s. Other community groups engaged their own
planning professionals or took legal action to appeal
projects inconsistent with neighborhood character.

Public concern for zoning and planning reform
grew in 2004 when the Building Industry Association
began advocating for changes to simplify the process
for obtaining permit approvals for new construction.
Their efforts were joined and enlarged by other organizations that felt that indiscriminate granting of
zoning variances reflected the lack of a guiding planning vision for Center City.

University of Pennsylvania expansion plan
2006
Sasaki Architects

As 2007 begins, planning for Center City is at a crossroads. The directions established by the 1963 and 1988 Center City plans have run their course and no new vision has emerged. Although the recent surge in residential development has contributed to a welcome growth in population and support for new restaurants and shopping, inappropriately sized residential projects have led neighborhood organizations to clamor for a reinvigorated planning function within government to insure a better balance between growth and preservation of existing scale and neighborhood character. So strong has been this concern that City Council recently approved first steps toward zoning reform.

On the other hand, there are new opportunities. Ambitious plans are under way for both the eastern and western edges of Center City. Office development has been initiated north of 30th Station, the area long contemplated as the next major site for commercial investment. The University of Pennsylvania has acquired the 30th Street Post Office and adjacent land to the south, with plans for an eastward expansion of its campus to the Schuylkill River, strengthening its connection to Center City. Along the Delaware River waterfront, Penn Praxis—the non-profit urban planning arm of the university's School of Design—has begun planning a comprehensive framework for waterfront development spurred in part by years of failed planning for Penn's Landing and by the siting of two casinos on the waterfront.

Complementing these large projects, Center City District has advanced planning concepts designed to balance Center City's intimate 18th- and 19th-century scale with the needs of 21st-century growth. One suggestion is to enhance the vitality of Center City resulting from recent residential growth by improving public plazas and parks to create vibrant public spaces. Another recognizes the importance of the quality of the pedestrian experience along routes linking major destinations. It suggests filling the "gaps in the fabric" along such corridors as Arch Street and Market Street from the Pennsylvania Convention Center to Independence Mall and along JFK Boulevard and West Market Street from the downtown office core to 30th Street Station. These ideas, combined with opportunities on both river-fronts, may provide the directions for the next Center City plan.

Proposal for redesign of Dilworth Plaza, Center City District

2007

Olin Partnership

When William Penn and Thomas Holme created the plan of Center City, it was set within the framework of a 500,000-acre region and a zone of Liberty Lands surrounding the city. In the centuries since, the region has grown extensively and lost its agricultural character. The Liberty Lands have become urbanized city neighborhoods, with no guiding plan, as a result of extensive growth in the 19th and early-20th centuries. The loss of population and manufacturing jobs hit these areas hardest; housing conditions declined and large tracts of land are now vacant. There is as much clamor for investment in neighborhood renewal and low- and moderate-income housing as for zoning reform.

Through all this change, the plan that Penn and Holme created for Center City has endured. It has enabled Center City Philadelphia to adapt to 325 years of changing circumstances and visions and become one of America's most distinctive urban environments.

P*hiladelphia planners have been influential in the practice of city planning since the profession was founded in the early-20th century. Some have been responsible for major planning efforts in Philadelphia while others made their major contributions to planning in other cities. The following nine people, all of who have lived and worked in Philadelphia, deserve special recognition for their contributions to the city and to the planning profession.*

Although neither William Penn nor Thomas Holme was a "planner," their efforts combined to produce a plan for Philadelphia of lasting significance.

WILLIAM PENN

William Penn was born to parents of relatively modest social position. However, by 1660 his father had become an admiral, a knighted member of the king's court, and a wealthy man with estates in Ireland. Penn attended Oxford, but was expelled for criticizing the Church of England. He then studied and traveled in France. Upon his return he studied law, attended court, and became friends with the king and his brother, the Duke of York.

Penn's life changed when he joined the Religious Society of Friends (Quakers) at the age of 23. He became an influential Quaker, writing over 50 books and pamphlets on Quaker issues. As a result of his religious beliefs, he spent several periods in jail. Penn's connection to the king's court made him an unusual religious leader; he eventually became the principal spokesperson not only for his own religious community, but also for other dissenting religious sects. He was instrumental in obtaining passage of

William Penn
1644–1718

Charter of Pennsylvania
1681

49

PHILADELPHIA PLANNERS

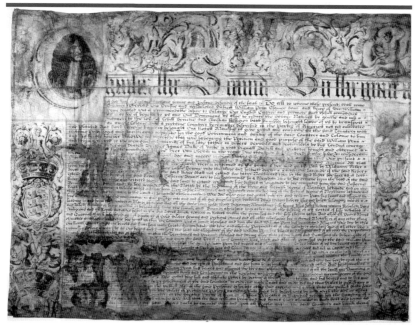

the Toleration Act in 1689 that give religious liberty to all Protestant sects in England.

Penn spent relatively little time in Pennsylvania. He came in 1682–84 to establish the plan and again in 1699–1701. During the latter period he created the Charter of Privileges that established the form of governance of the colony including the provision of freedom of worship and other legal rights not generally available in England. It would later influence the U.S. Constitution. Although the colony of Pennsylvania prospered, Penn never made money from his investment during his lifetime. He was on the verge of selling Pennsylvania back to the crown when he suffered a stroke in 1712 from which he never recovered.

THOMAS HOLME

Thomas Holme (1624–1695), 20 years younger than Penn, grew up in central England. He is believed to have joined Oliver Cromwell's army at 18 and remained in the army until several years after the war ended in Ireland. He became an active Quaker in 1656, when the war was over and he had left the army.

Soldiers who served in the army were paid for their services with land grants in Ireland. Holme worked on the surveys for these grants, which were conducted using the most advanced techniques of the time. Later, he was a small businessman, shipping goods back and forth between England and Barbados. Penn's offer of land in Pennsylvania attracted Holme as a business venture. He purchased land and was about to leave England for Pennsylvania with his family when Penn's first surveyor died and Penn selected him to become surveyor general. He held this position from 1681 to 1690 when he was almost blind and delegated most work to others. After a brief visit to England, he returned to Philadelphia and remained there until his death.

PAUL PHILIPPE CRET
1876–1945

Paul Philippe Cret was born in Lyons, France. He studied architecture at the Ecole des Beaux-Arts in Paris. Cret came to Philadelphia at the age of 27 to establish an Ecole system at the University of Pennsylvania. He held his teaching position for 34 years, during which time he revolutionized the architectural program and established the most successful Beaux-Arts curriculum in the country.

Cret served in the French army during World War I. Afterwards he established a thriving practice in Philadelphia and continued to devote himself to architectural education. He was predominantly an architect whose work honored the past, but was also influenced by the International style. Two of his major commissions were the Federal Reserve Bank of Philadelphia and the Folger Shakespeare Library in Washington, D.C., which Cret considered to be his finest work. He also designed the Delaware River Bridge (now the Benjamin Franklin Bridge) and a series of streamlined trains in the 1930s, including the Denver and Pioneer Zephyrs.

His interest in city planning involved him with Philadelphians interested in improving the physical environment. He was among a group of architects who advocated for a system of diagonal boulevards to connect the different parts of Philadelphia. In addition to preparing the original plans for the Benjamin Franklin Parkway, Cret conducted studies of other areas of the city including the Schuylkill River waterfront. He also redesigned Rittenhouse Square as part of a general improvement plan for the area.

PHILADELPHIA PLANNERS

Plan for Schuylkill River banks and 1926 Sesquicentennial

1924

Paul Philippe Cret

Jacques Greber
1882–1962

Jacques Greber was born in Paris, France. Like Paul Cret, he studied architecture at the Ecole des Beaux-Arts, graduating in 1908. Although Greber was an architect, he specialized in landscape architecture and urban design. In the period from 1910 to 1916 he designed many private gardens for wealthy clients. Joseph E. Widener brought him to Philadelphia in 1913 to design a French classical garden for "Lynnewood Hall," Widener's estate in Jenkintown. This led to collaboration with Horace Trumbauer, Widener's favorite architect, on several garden designs including those at "Whitemarsh Hall" in Montgomery County, the palatial estate of wealthy banker Edward T. Stotesbury.

Although Greber's best known plan is that of the Benjamin Franklin Parkway in Philadelphia, he practiced internationally. His other planning work included the 1937 Paris International Exposition, plans for Ottawa and the National Capital Region in Canada, and urban plans for the French cities of Marseille and Rouen. In 1929–30 he served as consultant to the Philadelphia City Planning Commission, helping to develop what was referred to as a "50-year plan" for Philadelphia.

His work in Philadelphia also includes the Rodin Museum, designed in collaboration with Paul Cret.

**Whitemarsh Hall
gardens**
1911

Edmund N. Bacon
1910–2005

Edmund Bacon was born in Philadelphia into a Quaker family. After completing his architecture degree at Cornell University in 1933, he used a $1,000 inheritance from his grandfather to travel. His visit to Beijing, China had a lasting influence on his concepts of architecture and planning.

Upon returning to the United States, he studied at Cranbrook Academy and then worked as a planner for the WPA in Flint, Michigan. He was brought back to Philadelphia by his friend Walter Phillips, who secured for Bacon the position of executive director of the Housing Association. Phillips also involved Bacon in the City Policy Committee, a group he formed that successfully advocated for the creation of professionally staffed city planning commission.

While serving in the U.S. Navy, Bacon began to develop ideas for an exhibition on city planning with Oskar Stonorov and Louis I. Kahn. The 1947 Better Philadelphia Exhibition inspired both citizens and civic leadership. Bacon became executive director of the City Planning Commission in 1949 and held that position until his retirement in 1970. During that period he attracted many talented young architects and planners to his staff and with their assistance developed a series of plans that would transform Center City. Although best known for these Center City plans, Bacon also created the plan that guided the development of the Far Northeast section of the city from farmland to a fully developed residential community. As a result of the success of his planning activities in Philadelphia, he was featured on the cover of *Time* Magazine in 1964.

After his retirement Bacon served as vice-president of Mondev U.S.A. and taught at several universities. He remained actively concerned about planning in Philadelphia and came out of retirement on several occasions to criticize subsequent planning, including the construction of office buildings taller than City Hall tower. At the age of 90, he criticized efforts to ban skateboarders from Love Park, adjacent to City Hall, and took to a skateboard himself in their defense.

Bacon described his ideas about urban form and planning in his book *Design of Cities,* published in 1967.

David A. Wallace
1918–2004

David Wallace grew up in Philadelphia from the age of two. He received degrees in architecture and city planning from the University of Pennsylvania and a master's degree and Ph.D. in city planning from Harvard University.

Wallace worked as a planner at the Chicago Housing Authority before becoming planning director for the Philadelphia Redevelopment Authority during the administration of Mayor Joseph S. Clark, Jr. After leaving that position, he achieved national prominence in 1955 with the design of Charles Center in downtown Baltimore for the Greater Baltimore Committee, considered one of the country's most successful urban renewal projects.

In 1963, Wallace and Ian McHarg founded Wallace McHarg Roberts and Todd (now Wallace, Roberts & Todd LLC), which became one of the most prominent planning and urban design firms in the country. Shortly after establishing the firm, Wallace produced the master plan for the Baltimore Inner Harbor. The Inner Harbor plan was instrumental in transforming downtown Baltimore and drew the attention of cities throughout the country to the potential of waterfront development. Up to his retirement in 1991, Wallace was involved in major award-winning planning projects throughout the world.

Wallace developed a systematic approach to planning and urban design that evaluated the probability for change in relation to existing conditions and provided a design response. He was an influential teacher first at the University of Chicago and then from 1962 to 1979 at the University of Pennsylvania. Wallace described his approach to planning in his book *Urban Planning/My Way*, which was published in 2004.

Inner Harbor,
Baltimore, MD

IAN L. McHARG
1920–2001

Ian McHarg, a pioneer in environmental and regional planning, was born and raised outside of Glasgow, Scotland. McHarg served as a paratrooper during the Second World War, after which he entered the Harvard University Graduate School of Design, receiving degrees in both landscape architecture and city planning. He worked in Scotland as a planner before being invited back to the United States to teach at the University of Pennsylvania. McHarg co-founded Penn's Department of Landscape Architecture and Regional Planning and served as its chair from 1955 to 1986. His course, "Man and the Environment," was one of the most popular in the university and later became a 12-part television series called *The House We Live In.*

In 1963, he co-founded the firm of Wallace McHarg Roberts and Todd with David Wallace and remained a partner until 1981. His planning work pioneered an ecological approach to the design of urban, metropolitan and rural regions. McHarg's 1969 book *Design With Nature* (reprinted 1992) is considered to be one of the most influential books of the ecological movement. He also authored two other books, including *Quest for Life* (1996), his autobiography.

55

**Plan for the Valleys,
Baltimore, MD**

1963

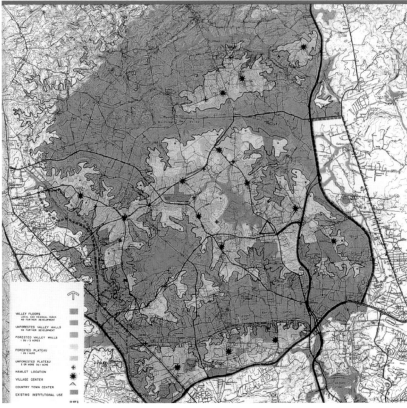

DAVID A. CRANE
1927–2005

David A. Crane was born in the former Belgian Congo, where his parents were missionaries. After returning to the United States, he enlisted in the US Navy at 17, following which he studied architecture at Georgia Institute of Technology. He received a master's degree in city planning from Harvard University in 1952.

Crane achieved national prominence while working with Edward J. Logue as chief planner for the Boston Redevelopment Authority from 1961 to 1965. He created urban renewal plans for many of Boston's most important projects including the Government Center, the South End, Charlestown and the city's waterfront. His concept of urban planning focused on the design of what he referred to as the "capital web"—the collective infrastructure of all public systems and facilities.

From 1957 to 1972, Crane was affiliated with the Department of City and Regional Planning of the University of Pennsylvania. His interest in architecture and planning led him to help create at Penn one of the nation's first urban design programs. Subsequently, he was dean of the School of Architecture at Rice University in Houston, Texas, and from 1986 to 2002 he was on the faculty of the South Florida School of Architecture and Community Design.

Crane established a private planning practice in Philadelphia in 1970, now Kise Straw Kolodner. Much of his early work focused on the development of new towns. He planned several new towns for the New York State Urban Development Corporation and participated in the planning of Sadat City, a new town outside of Cairo, Egypt.

Fort Lincoln New Town "capital web"

1977

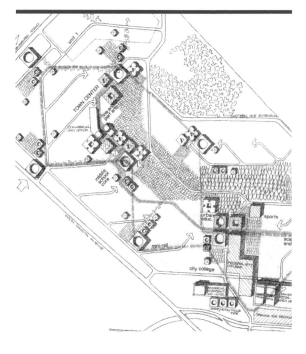

DENISE SCOTT BROWN
1931–

Denise Scott Brown was born in Nkana, Zambia. After studying at the University of Witwatesrand in South Africa, she moved to London in 1952 to study at the Architectural Association then came to the United States in 1958 to first study and then teach at the University of Pennsylvania. It was there she met her future husband and collaborator, Robert Venturi.

In 1967, Scott Brown joined the firm now called Venturi Scott Brown and Associates as director of planning. Early projects included plans for Philadelphia's South Street, Miami Beach, and Memphis. Recently Scott Brown has focused on university planning and design using tools evolved by melding methods of architecture and planning. Her projects have included campus planning for Dartmouth College, Williams College, the University of Michigan, and the Radcliffe Institute for Advanced Studies at Harvard. She also participates in the development of the firm's architectural projects for which she uses urban analysis and planning concepts to create programs and shape architectural designs.

Scott Brown is an influential educator and prolific writer. She has taught at Berkeley and at Yale, Harvard and Princeton universities and lectured at other universities throughout the world. Her books, written in collaboration with Robert Venturi, have broadened the practice of architecture and planning to recognize the influence of popular culture and the everyday landscape. *Learning from Las Vegas*, written in 1972 with Robert Venturi and Steven Izenour, expressed ideas about architecture and urban design that have had international influence.

University of Michigan Life Sciences Complex showing linkages
2003

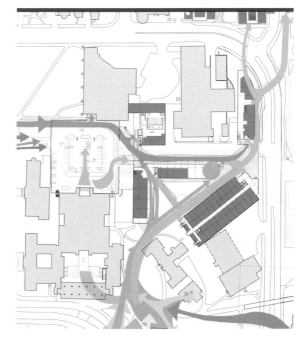

Liberty Bell Center

2003

6th and Market streets
Bohlin Cywinski Jackson
Open to the public

Tours

Introduction

The plan of Philadelphia created by William Penn and his surveyor, Thomas Holme, covered the area between the Delaware and Schuylkill rivers, from the present Vine to South streets. Today this area is known as Center City.

The current form of Center City was shaped by the plan Penn and Holme designed, and by the modifications that came about as the city grew and new businesses and civic institutions were created. No new plans were made for Center City until the late 19th century when the idea of the Benjamin Franklin Parkway was proposed. The Parkway, an outstanding example of the City Beautiful movement in the United States, was not completed until the early 20th century. Ambitious plans for other parts of Center City were proposed in the 1920s and 1930s, but never implemented. Many of these early-20th-century plans were revived, redesigned, augmented and initiated after 1950 with funding from the federal urban renewal program. The plans created during this period shaped the growth and development of Center City for the remainder of the century.

The results of these different eras of planning can be seen most easily in the five areas of Center City covered by the following walking tours. Each tour can be taken separately or linked to others for a longer tour.

The first two tours cover the oldest sections of the city—Old City and Society Hill. Within these areas the pat-

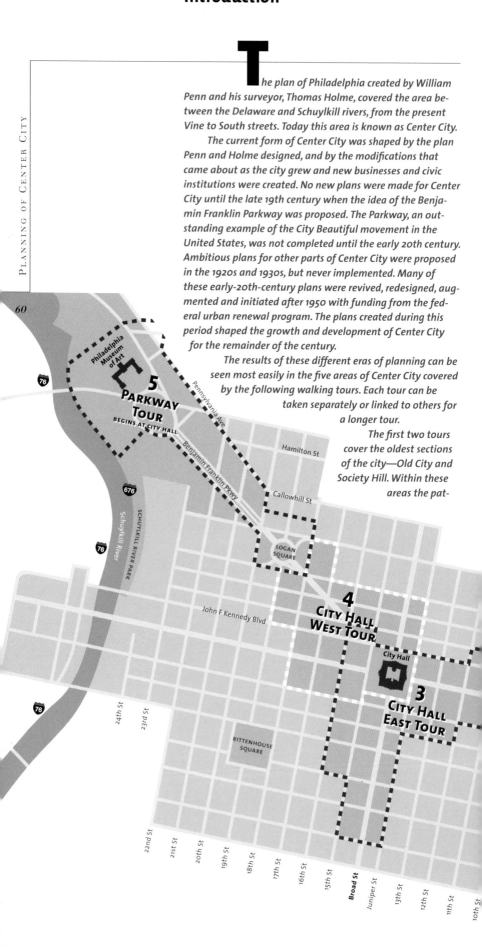

60

Philadelphia Museum of Art

5 PARKWAY TOUR
BEGINS AT CITY HALL

Pennsylvania Ave

Benjamin Franklin Pkwy

Hamilton St

Callowhill St

LOGAN SQUARE

Schuylkill River

SCHUYLKILL RIVER PARK

John F Kennedy Blvd

4 CITY HALL WEST TOUR

City Hall

3 CITY HALL EAST TOUR

RITTENHOUSE SQUARE

24th St · 23rd St · 22nd St · 21st St · 20th St · 19th St · 18th St · 17th St · 16th St · 15th St · Broad St · Juniper St · 13th St · 12th St · 11th St · 10th St

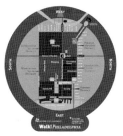

tern of the original plan of the city and the development it fostered are most visible. Both areas show the influence of mid-20th-century planning as well. The Old City tour connects to Independence Mall, one of the major planning efforts of the urban renewal period that was re-planned again in 1999–2000. The two tours connect at Independence National Historical Park.

The tours east and west of City Hall show the results of mid-20th-century planning for retail and office development, and late-20th-century planning for a cultural district along South Broad Street. The tour of the Parkway, a monument to the early-20th-century City Beautiful movement, extends from City Hall to the Philadelphia Museum of Art and nearby historic sites that were among the most popular places visited by tourists in the 19th century.

In addition to having an important place in the history of planning, Philadelphia—more than any other American city—exemplifies the history of architecture in the United States. Many of the city's landmark buildings are located in Center City in the areas covered by the five tours. The best buildings in each area are indicated by numbers preceding the building name in the text, with corresponding numbers on the tour maps. Each of these buildings is illustrated and described. Other noteworthy buildings along the tour route are indicated by letters and briefly described.

Each tour begins and ends at a station on the Market-Frankford subway line. Each area can also be reached by the many bus routes that traverse Center City. Bus kiosks at street corners display the Center City District's map of bus routes, which also illustrates and describes the past history of the immediate area. For the tour of the Benjamin Franklin Parkway—a one-mile walk from City Hall to the Art Museum —the Phlash bus provides an alternative means of transportation in summer with stops at City Hall, Logan Circle and the Art Museum.

There are many cultural institutions and other historic sites within each tour area that are not noted on the tour maps. The Center City District's wayfinding signs and maps, located at the corner and in the center of most blocks, respectively, identify the important sites in each neighborhood and provide direction to their location.

INTRODUCTION

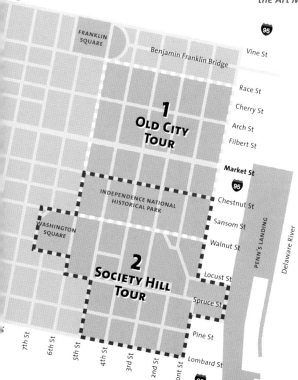

Old City and Independence Mall Tour

The first settlers in Philadelphia lived in caves in the bluff above the Delaware River while they cleared the lots assigned to them by Penn's surveyor, Thomas Holme. The first permanent settlement was located on the high ground between Walnut Street and Vine Street, slowly extending back to 4th Street as the city grew. Old City, as this area is now known, was the first residential area in Philadelphia and contained the city's earliest houses, religious and civic buildings. Second and Market streets was the center of the city; around this intersection were located the Great Quaker Meetinghouse, the Courthouse and townhall, the jail, the primary Anglican Church and the city markets, which initially extended from Front to 3rd streets.

As Philadelphia grew westward, Old City gradually lost its popularity as a residential neighborhood. Proximity to the port encouraged merchants to build warehouses and commercial buildings, and the markets were extended further west. By the end of the 19th century, many of the institutions and most of houses were gone. Now the area is noteworthy for its fine examples of 18th- and 19th-century commercial buildings of different architectural styles and materials ranging from brick, terra cotta and marble to cast iron.

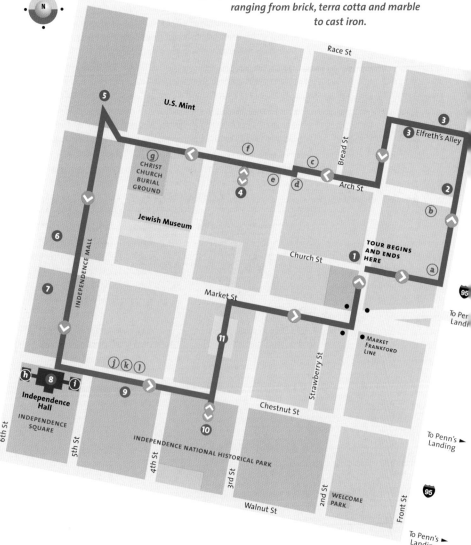

2nd Street North from Market Street

1800

Wm. Birch & Son

In the mid-20th century, Old City changed again. The investment tax credits for rehabilitation of historic properties provided by the Tax Reform Act of 1976 prompted the creation of a plan for the revitalization of Old City. The plan demonstrated how the new tax credits could be used to finance the conversion of what were then marginally used commercial buildings to residential use. Old City was designated a National Register Historic District in 1980, following which hundreds of new apartments were created in former commercial loft buildings. From a population of 225 in 1970, the area grew to 2,650 residents by the 2000 Census. This transformation attracted many new businesses, including a concentration of art galleries and restaurants, which in turn encouraged the construction of new condominium buildings. As a result, Old City once again became a vibrant residential neighborhood.

Independence Mall in 1950 before demolition

Just west of Old City is the Independence Mall area, one of the major urban renewal projects of the mid-20th century.

By 1750, the developed area of Philadelphia had not extended past 5th Street. As residential development shifted south from Old City to Society Hill, the commerce and businesses that over-

took Old City gradually expanded past 5th Street following the western growth of the city markets along Market Street. What is now the Independence Mall area (5th Street to 6th Street, Race to Chestnut streets) was once a dense concentration of brick, terra cotta and cast iron commercial buildings much like Old City.

As early as 1923, plans were proposed for the creation of a "court of honor" called Constitution Place north of Independence Hall. This was expanded in 1936 to a plan for a mall from Chestnut to Vine streets that would create a proper setting for Independence Hall, as well as include locations for apartment houses, offices and theaters. The plan for the mall *was revived in the early 1940s and a plan for a three-block-long formal park adopted. This became the centerpiece of one of the major planning projects of the 1950–60 urban renewal period. The Commonwealth of Pennsylvania acquired and demolished all the buildings in the blocks between 5th and 6th streets from Chestnut to Race streets beginning in 1953 and the City acquired and demolished properties east of 5th Street and west of 6th Street to create sites for new office buildings. Today the west side of 6th Street is lined by the office buildings of the Federal Reserve Bank, the Federal Office Building and Courthouse and the Rohm and Haas Company (6th and Market streets), the first office building built on the mall.*

The design of the mall completed in 1965 consisted of three blocks of park and public plazas. In 1999, the National Park Service retained the Olin Partnership to redesign the mall, at which time the amount of park space was reduced and three sites designated for new buildings—the National Constitution Center, the Independence Visitor Center, and the Liberty Bell Center.

To reach the start of the Old City and Independence Mall tour take the Market-Frankford subway line or a bus on Market or Chestnut streets to 2nd Street.

The tour begins at 2nd and Market streets, once the center of Philadelphia. To begin the tour, walk north on 2nd Street a short half-block and turn left on Church Street, which is paved in cobblestones, as were many Old City streets.

First on the tour is **Christ Church**, the only remaining example of the cluster of civic buildings that were concentrated near 2nd and Market streets in colonial times.

Although Penn founded Philadelphia to provide a refuge for Quakers, he extended freedom of worship to all religions. One of the first groups to exercise this right was the Anglicans of the Church of England. They first constructed a small, wood-frame building on this site and later replaced it with a new church modeled on the work of Sir Christopher Wren, the English architect who rebuilt 52 churches in London after the Great Fire.

Christ Church was the most sumptuous building in the colonies. Construction was supervised by John Kearsley, a physician, who was one of the first of many gentlemen-architects who designed important civic buildings. Robert Smith, the most prominent master carpenter of the time, worked on the 196-foot-high steeple, which was added in 1751–54. The brick tower was finished quickly, but it took three lotteries, sponsored by Benjamin Franklin, to raise enough money to add the wooden part. Christ Church is considered to have been the tallest building in America for 100 years.

From Christ Church cross 2nd Street and continue east on Church Street to Front Street. The Penn/Holme plan did not include the narrow streets and alleys that now exist between the major numbered and named streets. Early settlers

❶

Christ Church
1727–44
2nd and Market streets
Dr. John Kearsley, supervisor
Open to the public

found their lots larger than they needed and houses too far apart. Lots were sub-divided and new streets introduced to allow development of housing for rent to later settlers. Church Street, Cuthbert Street and Elfreth's Alley (all located between Front and Second streets) are examples of these early alleys.

At Front Street, turn left and walk one block north to Arch Street.

The block of Front Street between Church and Arch streets is the last remaining intact block of the 19th-century commercial buildings that once extended from Vine to Walnut streets and provided the principal view of the city to arriving ships. Now the view to and from the river is blocked by the high wall of Interstate 95, the result of mid-20th-century transportation planning. The commercial buildings at ⓐ **20–50 North Front Street** were built for Stephen Girard, one of the city's most prominent businessmen and the wealthiest man in America when he died in 1831. After being vacant for decades, they were planned for condominiums in 2006.

On the northwest corner of Front and Arch streets is the ❷ **Smythe Buildings**, one of the many commercial buildings converted to residential use following the passage of the Tax Reform Act of 1976 and the designation of Old City as a National Register Historic District. The facade of the Smythe Buildings is the best example of cast-iron design remaining in Philadelphia. It originally extended half a block with a continuous facade composed of the delicate cast-iron columns and arched windows.

On the south side of the street is ⓑ **108 Arch Street** (2004), Bower Lewis Thrower/SHoP, architects, one of the new mid-rise condominium buildings whose impact on the historic character of the neighborhood led to the imposition of a height limit for new construction in 2005.

Continue walking north on Front Street and turn left onto ❸ **Elfreth's Alley**. Elfreth's Alley, the oldest continuously inhabited street in the country, is an example of the way early settlers modified the Penn/Holme plan. It was created in 1703 when two property owners on Front Street made a cartway to the rear of their lots to subdivide their land. Most of the houses were built for rent and lived in by craftsmen. The Museum House at 126 (open to the public) is typical of these early homes. It was occupied by a dressmaker who had her shop in the front room on the first floor and living quarters above.

The walk down Elfreth's Alley ends at 2nd Street. Turn left and walk to Arch Street and then turn right and proceed past 3rd Street. Along the way you will pass the ⓒ **Betsy Ross House** (1740), 239 Arch Street, which is similar in

Smythe Buildings
1855–57
101–111 Arch Street
Private residences

Elfreth's Alley
from 1720
2nd Street above Arch Street
Private residences

character, scale and design to the oldest houses on Elfreth's Alley.

At the corner of 3rd and Arch streets are two fine examples of cast iron architecture. On the southeast corner is ⓓ **Merchants Row**, 63 North 3rd Street, an 1852 commercial building with an Italianate-style cast iron facade. It and several adjacent buildings were converted to condominiums in 2004. On the southwest corner is the ⓔ **St. Charles Hotel** (1851), 60–66 North 3rd Street, Charles Rubican, builder. The facade is actually cast iron but it was painted with sand added to the paint to create the color and texture of stone. It is another of the buildings converted to apartments following the Tax Reform Act of 1976.

Just past 3rd Street on the left is the ❹ **Arch Street**

Friends Meetinghouse. William Penn and many of the original settlers of Philadelphia were members of the Religious Society of Friends, commonly known as Quakers. The meetinghouses built for their services usually contained two rooms: a large entrance and gathering room and the meeting room itself.

The Arch Street Meetinghouse is the largest in the city and second oldest. There are two rooms in the central structure and two flanking wings that were used for annual meetings when men and women met separately. The plain brick structure with flat exterior surfaces and limited ornamentation is evidence of the Quaker commitment to simplicity.

Arch Street Friends Meetinghouse

1803–05/1810–11

330 Arch Street
Owen Biddle
Open to the public

❺

National Constitution Center

2000–2003

Arch Street,
5th to 6th streets
Pei Cobb Freed & Partners
Open to the public

After visiting the Meetinghouse, return to Arch Street. Directly opposite the Meetinghouse is ⓕ **Loxley Court** (1744), 321–323 Arch Street, another example of the colonial houses still remaining in Old City. Benjamin Franklin used the key from Number 2 Loxley Court for his famous kite experiment with lightning.

Turn left on Arch Street and proceed to 5th Street. At the corner of 5th and Arch streets is ⓖ **the Christ Church Burial Ground**. Christ Church purchased this plot of land in 1719 on what was then the outskirts of town. Over 5,000 people are buried here including Benjamin Franklin.

Cross 5th Street to the north side of Arch Street and enter the Independence Mall area. On the north side of Arch Street is the ❺ **National Constitution Center**. The Constitution Center is dedicated to

increasing public understanding of the U.S. Constitution. It contains interactive exhibits, photographs, sculpture, film and artifacts that tell the story of the Constitution. The low Indiana limestone and glass building terminates the northern end of the mall and provides a contrast to Independence Hall to the south.

From the Constitution Center, cross Arch Street and walk through the mall to 6th and Market streets.

Among the new buildings added when the mall was redesigned is the **Independence Visitor Center**. The Visitors Center extends along the entire western edge of the second block of the mall. Its brick piers, tall porches and vine-covered trellises are intended to great a "garden wall" to the park. The narrow Market Street frontage contains a gift shop on the first floor with an expansive outdoor viewing terrace on the second.

Cross Market Street at 6th Street to the **Liberty Bell Center**.

Independence Visitor Center
2002
6th and Market streets
Kallman, McKinnell & Wood
Open to the public

67

Liberty Bell Center
2003
6th and Market streets
Bohlin Cywinski Jackson
Open to the public

The Liberty Bell Center is the third of the new buildings constructed when the mall was redesigned. The Liberty Bell was cast in 1753 and originally hung in the tower of Independence Hall. The name is derived from the biblical inscription on the bell, "Proclaim liberty throughout all the land unto all the inhabitants thereof." The pavilion for the bell is set at an angle to Chestnut Street to provide an unobstructed view past the tower of Independence Hall.

Continue through the mall to Chestnut Street and the Independence National Historical Park. The National Park was authorized by Congress in 1948 and established in 1956. The creation of the park was part of the mid-20th-century planning for the transformation of the historic sections of eastern Center City. Many buildings—including outstanding examples of 19th-century architecture—were demolished to create a landscape setting for the key historic buildings related to the founding of the nation, of which Independence Hall is the focal point.

Between 5th and 6th streets along Chestnut Street is the **⑧ Independence Hall complex**. The complex consists of the State House, built for the Pennsylvania legislature, and Congress Hall and the Supreme Court building, both added after the Revolutionary War.

In 1729, Philadelphia lawmakers decided to move the government from the cramped quarters of the Town Hall at 2nd and Market streets to a site at Chestnut Street between 5th and 6th streets even though it was on the outskirts of town. The decision would influence the growth of the city for the next hundred years. The State House is an outstanding example of Georgian design. It was modified in 1750, when the Assembly voted to commemorate the 50 years of Penn's Charter of Privileges by adding a tower to the rear. At the same time, a large clock was built against the west end of the building. The long case, made of rusticated stone, hid the weights and lines necessary for an eight-day clock.

In 1830, John Haviland, the Greek Revival architect, undertook the first of many restorations of the building. In 1950, the National Park Service conducted an archeological study, which provided the information necessary to restore the State House to its 1776 appearance.

The two buildings flanking Independence Hall are ⓗ **Congress Hall** (1787–89) and the ⓘ **U.S. Supreme Court** (1790–91). Although planned as early as 1736, these two buildings were not built until after the Revolutionary War. After the federal government left Philadelphia in 1800, Congress Hall became Philadelphia's City Hall.

⑧

Independence Hall (State House)

1732–48

Chestnut Street,
5th to 6th streets
Alexander Hamilton
with Edmund Wooley
Open to the public

The National Park Service gives tours of the Independence Hall complex and other buildings in the park.

Cross 5th Street and proceed east along Chestnut Street.

In the middle of the south side of the block is the **⑨ Second Bank of the United States**. The Second Bank was founded in 1816. When the bank held a competition for the design of its new building, Nicholas Biddle, president of the bank, required all architects to use the Greek style. William Strickland's design, modeled after the Parthenon in Athens, is one of the first Greek Revival public buildings in the country.

This portion of Chestnut Street was the city's financial district in the 19th century. Many of the original bank buildings have been demolished and those that remain have been converted to other uses. The most noteworthy remaining buildings are located on the north side of the street. They include the ⓙ **Pennsylvania Company for Insurances on**

⑨

Second Bank of the United States

1818–24

420 Chestnut Street
William Strickland
Open to the public

Carpenters' Hall

1770–74

320 Chestnut Street
Robert Smith
Open to the public

Lives and Granting Annuities (1871–73), 431 Chestnut Street, Addison Hutton; the (k) **Farmers' and Mechanics' Bank** (1854–55), 427 Chestnut Street, John M. Gries; and the (l) **Bank of Pennsylvania** (1857–59), 421 Chestnut Street, John M. Gries.

Continue to walk east, crossing 4th Street. In the middle of the block is **10 Carpenters' Hall**.

In the 18th century, building trades in the city were dominated by members of the Carpenters' Company, founded in 1724. In addition to building design and construction, members assisted contractors and clients in determining the fair value of completed work. Robert Smith, a member, was chosen to design the company's meeting place. He created a cruciform plan based on one of Palladio's Italian villas and the town halls of his native Scotland. The members used the hall for their meetings, but also rented space to other organizations. The most famous group to use the hall was the Continental Congress in 1774.

Directly opposite Carpenters' Hall on the north side of Chestnut Street is a small street that leads to **11 Franklin Court**.

Benjamin Franklin built his own house and print shop in the courtyard behind a row of tenant buildings on Market

69

Franklin Court

restored 1973–76

312–22 Market Street
Venturi and Rauch, with
John Milner Associates
Open to the public

Street. Although the tenant buildings survived, Franklin's house, except for sections of foundations, was destroyed. Lacking sufficient evidence to reconstruct the house faithfully, the National Park Service commissioned the architects to design an interpretative complex.

The most original aspect of the design is the white tubular-steel frames outlining Franklin's original buildings. The plans of the house and print shop are inlaid in the paving beneath the frames, supplemented by quotes from Franklin and his wife cut into the slate paving. Beneath the ghost structure and 18th-century garden is a museum that contains imaginative exhibits about Franklin's life and accomplishments.

To continue on to the Society Hill tour (page 70) exit back to Chestnut Street. To complete the Old City tour leave Franklin Court by the archway on the north through the tenant buildings to Market Street, turn right and return to 2nd Street. This portion of Market Street once contained market sheds that filled the middle of the street. Produce and other goods were brought here from all over the city. The sheds ultimately extended as far west as 12th Street and were not demolished until 1859. Today the area contains an eclectic mix of restaurants and stores that makes Old City a popular destination.

The Old City Tour ends at 2nd and Market streets.

Society Hill and Independence National Historical Park Tour

When ships first came to Philadelphia they landed in Dock Creek, a natural inlet south of Walnut Street. The original commercial center of the city began here, but quickly moved north to Market Street. Residential develop-

Dock Street markets
1920

ment west of the inlet began early, but the area did not become well developed until the 1740s when more affluent families wanted larger houses, free from the mix of commercial uses found in Old City. As one of the principal residential areas of colonial Philadelphia, the neighborhood included homes of the wealthy and poor, prominent churches, markets and taverns. Today Society Hill contains the largest concentration of original 18th-century architecture of any place in the United States.

As the city grew westward in the 19th century, the affluent population followed and Society Hill became a neighborhood of immigrants many of whom worked in businesses along the waterfront. Proximity to the port encouraged the same type of commercial development that occurred in Old City. By the end of the 19th century, Dock Creek had vanished and the area was dominated by wholesale food distribution businesses serving the Philadelphia region. Colonial houses were converted to shops, small factories and rooming houses. Although a vibrant immigrant neighborhood, the physical condition of the area had so deteriorated that by the early 20th century, Society Hill was thought to be a slum and in need of restoration.

Plans for the revival of the area were first put forward in 1929 when Mayor Harry Mackey proposed that the area be redeveloped for working class families. However, nothing happened until the 1950s, when the wholesale food market that dominated the area was relocated and the federal urban renewal program provided the funds required to acquire deteriorated properties. Society Hill became the centerpiece of Center City's revival and the first urban renewal project in the nation to incorporate historic preservation. Eighteenth-century buildings were restored and 19th-century buildings demolished. A system of pedestrian greenways was introduced and where sites were available for new residential construction the best modern design was encouraged. It was at this time that the neighborhood was named Society Hill after the 18th-century Society of Free Traders, which had its offices on the hill above Dock Creek.

The easiest way to reach the Society Hill tour is to take a Market or Chestnut Street bus or the Market-Frankford subway line to 5th Street.

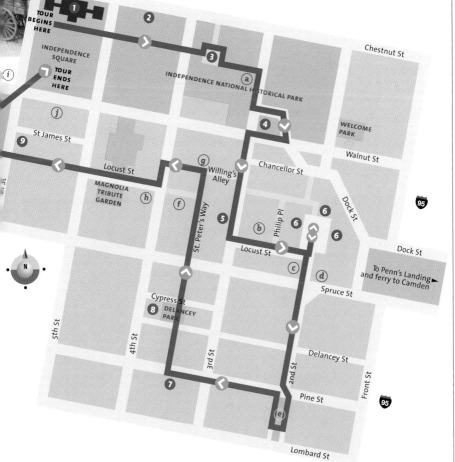

The tour begins at Independence Square, proceeds through the Independence National Historical Park and then through Society Hill, returning to Independence Square.

The first three buildings on the tour—**①Independence Hall**, the **②Second Bank of the United States** and **③Carpenters' Hall**—are also included on the Old City tour. See pages 68–69 for descriptions of these buildings.

After leaving Carpenters' Hall, continue east through the National Park to 3rd Street, then turn right and walk past the ⓐ **First Bank of the United States** (1795–97/1901), 120 South 3rd Street, Samuel Blodgett and James Windrim, architects. This was the first national bank in the country, created by Alexander Hamilton, and the most imposing structure of its day.

At the corner of 3rd and Walnut streets is the **④Merchants' Exchange**.

When Philadelphia businesses became too numerous to meet in coffeehouses and taverns, merchants formed the Philadelphia Exchange Company. The building consists of a rectangular main building and a semi-circular portico. The Exchange Room, in the portico, was sumptuous. It had a mosaic floor and a domed ceiling supported on marble columns. The Exchange dissolved during the Civil War. When wholesale food markets took over the area, sheds were erected around the east end of the building. These remained until 1952, when the Exchange was purchased by the National Park Service and adapted for its offices.

Merchants' Exchange
1832–33
143 South 3rd Street
William Strickland

Powel House
1765
244 South 3rd Street
Open to the public

After walking around the Merchants' Exchange, proceed south on 3rd Street, passing from the Independence National Historical Park into the Society Hill residential neighborhood. On the right at 244 South 3rd Street is the **⑤Powel House**.

The Powel House is the finest Georgian rowhouse in the city. It is representative of the larger houses that were built by the more affluent families as they moved south from Old City. Samuel Powel, its second owner, was the first mayor of Philadelphia after the Revolution. Powel was a Quaker who later turned Anglican. This change can be seen in his house. The restrained exterior reflects the Quaker concern for simplicity. Inside, restraint gives way to luxurious rooms decorated with fine paneling, elaborate carving and delicate plasterwork. Robert Smith, the prominent carpenter-architect, worked on this interior.

Cross 3rd Street to the east side and then proceed east on Locust Walk to the ⓑ Society Hill Townhouses (1962) and the **⑥Society Hill Towers**.

When the wholesale food markets that previously occupied the Dock Street area were relocated to a

6

Society Hill Towers
1964

200 Locust Street
I. M. Pei and Associates
Private residences

St. Peter's Church
1758–61

3rd and Pine streets
Robert Smith,
carpenter-architect
Open to the public

new food distribution center in the 1950s, a large site became available for new residential development. A competition was held to select a housing design that would symbolize the renewal of the area. I. M. Pei's winning entry included the townhouses on 3rd Street, the three tall apartment buildings located on the axis of 2nd Street and two additional towers on the east side of Washington Square.

The townhouses provide a transition between the towers and the 18th- and 19th-century rowhouses on 3rd Street. The three-story houses with dark brick facades are clustered around a landscaped parking court. The towers are constructed of poured-in-place concrete, divided into meticulous rectilinear units that are both the structural frame and the facade. Each apartment has floor-to-ceiling glass windows, which provide dramatic views of the river and the city. The entrance court contains the sculptural group *Old Man, Young Man, The Future* by Leonard Baskin.

Looking east from the courtyard of the towers, the shape of the original Dock Creek can be seen in the Belgian block paved street in the foreground. Beyond is a landscaped covered deck over Interstate 95—one of the major planning struggles of the 1960s—that leads to Penn's Landing, another of the major planning projects of the mid-20th century. All the piers and wharfs in the area from South Street to Arch Street were removed and a site created for public plazas, museums and historic ships.

From the Towers, walk south on 2nd Street past the **©** **Abercrombie House** (1759), 268–70 South 2nd Street, a fine example of Georgian residential design, and the **ⓓ Man Full of Trouble Tavern** (1760), 127 Spruce Street. In colonial times, taverns were places for socializing and conducting business. This one had rooms for travelers on the second floor and in the attic, whose gambrel roof gave more room than the common pitched roof.

Continue south on 2nd Street to Pine Street and the **ⓔ Head House and Market Shed** (1745/1804), which was the city's second market, built to serve the growing population of Society Hill. These are the oldest buildings of their kind in the country. The shed provided stalls for farmers to set up carts and, by 1777, extended to South Street. The Head House at Pine Street was added in 1804. It housed fire apparatus and served as a meeting place for volunteer fire companies.

After walking around the Market Shed, return to Pine Street and turn left, proceeding along Pine past 3rd Street to **❼ St. Peter's Church**.

By 1750, Christ Church at 2nd and Market streets could no longer accommodate the number of people who wanted to have seats there, many of whom now lived south of Walnut Street. The Penn family donated land for a second Anglican church, the "chapel of ease" as St. Peter's was first called. Robert Smith designed and

73

built the church. Dr. John Kearsley, who had directed work on Christ Church, was the supervisor. The steeple was added in 1852 by William Strickland. The simple tower, six stories high, is in keeping with the church's restrained exterior.

Across from St. Peter's is one of the many landscaped pedestrian greenways that are a distinctive feature of the Society Hill plan.

Take the greenway to Delancey Street. Delancey Street from 2nd to 4th streets is an excellent example of the results of the urban renewal program of the 1960s. Twentieth-century modern houses are interspersed among beautifully restored colonial houses. The greenway system crosses Delancey Street, connecting from St. Peter's Church through Three Bears Park past Spruce Street to Bingham Court. Before continuing on, notice the **❽ Hill-Physick-Keith House**. This is the only remaining example of the many freestanding mansions that once existed within the rowhouse fabric of Society Hill. It is also one of the finest examples of Federal-style architecture. Colonel Henry Hill, a prosperous wine merchant, built the house, which was later owned by Dr. Philip Syng Physick, the father of American surgery. The spacious interior contains 32 rooms, including a ballroom on the first floor finished with elaborate woodwork.

❽

Hill-Physick-Keith House
1786
321 South 4th Street
Open to the public

Leaving the Hill-Physick-Keith House, continue north along the greenway (St. Peters Way) across Spruce Street to Bingham Court. On St. Peter's Way just north of Spruce Street is a commemorative marker to Edmund Bacon and Charles Peterson, the two individuals thought to be most responsible for the planning and restoration of Society Hill. **ⓕ Bingham Court** (1967), also designed by I. M. Pei, is another example of the modern residential development encouraged during the urban renewal period. Go through Bingham Court to Willings Alley. Through the narrow archway is **ⓖ Old St. Josephs Church**, (1839), 321 Willings Alley. This is the third structure on this site, the first being a 1733 chapel that was the first Roman Catholic place of worship in Philadelphia. At that time, this was the only place in the English-speaking world where the offering of the Catholic mass was permitted by law.

Turn left on Willings Alley back to 4th Street, then left to Locust Street. On the corner of 4th and Locust streets is the **ⓗ Shippen-Wistar House** (1765) 238 South 4th Street, another of the lavish mansions typical of the colonial period.

Cross 4th Street and proceed along Locust Street. On the left is the Magnolia Tribute Garden, contributed to the National Park by the Garden Club of America, and on the right is a pedestrian greenway that leads back to Independence National Historical Park. Past 4th Street, Locust Street becomes Locust Walk, passing beside Independence Place, the second site designated for high-rise apartment buildings in the Society Hill plan, and the Lippincott Building, another of the many former commercial buildings converted to condominiums in recent years. Right next door at 221 South 6th Street is the home of former Mayor Richardson Dilworth, who led the efforts to revitalize Society Hill and built this Colonial Revival house in 1957 as evidence of his personal commitment to the redevelopment of the neighborhood. Adjacent to it is ⑨ **The Athenaeum of Philadelphia**.

The Athenaeum of Philadelphia
1845
219 South 6th Street
John Notman

In 1814 a group of young men formed a social and literary club and named it after Athena, the goddess of wisdom and learning. Their building was the first Renaissance Revival building in America. It was one of the earliest uses of brownstone as a building material. Both the design and material influenced a number of later residences and clubs in the city.

Cross 6th Street into Washington Square. Washington Square was one of the five squares set aside in the original Penn/Holme plan. In the colonial period, the square was used for a variety of purposes: for grazing animals, as a potter's field, a burial ground for troops from the Colonial army and for camp meetings. It was a gathering place for African American freemen and slaves and was also known as Congo Square. It was named after George Washington in 1825 and contains the Tomb of the Unknown Soldier of the Revolutionary War. In the 19th century, the square was surrounded by major publishing companies, including the Curtis Publishing Company whose headquarters was located in the building on the north side of the square.

Leave the park at 6th and Walnut streets. Before returning to Independence Square go into the lobby of the ⓘ **Curtis Building** (1910), Edgar Seeler, architect, and see *The Dream Garden*, an extraordinary 49-foot long colored glass mosaic created in 1914 by Louis Comfort Tiffany from a design by Maxfield Parrish. It contains over 100,000 pieces of glass in 260 color tones. After exiting, take note of the distinctive ⓙ **Penn Mutual Life Insurance Co. Addition** (1969–70), 510 Walnut Street, Mitchell/Giurgola Associates. The design incorporates the 1838 Egyptian Revival facade of John Haviland's Pennsylvania Fire Insurance Company.

The tour ends in Independence Square.

City Hall East Tour

As the city grew further west, the market sheds along High Street—as Market Street was known until 1859—followed, reaching 8th Street by the 1820s and 12th Street some years later. Other business located along the street adjacent to the markets including the city's first department store, founded in 1871. Even after the sheds were demolished in 1859, the markets remained in market halls in the area. The concentration of retail shopping was reinforced by the construction of the Reading Railroad's new terminal at 12th Street in 1893. By the early 1900s, there were five department stores surrounded by numerous smaller stores along Market Street from 7th Street to City Hall.

Suburban growth in the 1950s along with new suburban shopping malls drew customers away from Market Street. A plan for the revitalization of the area was proposed in the 1963 Center City Plan, but not begun until 1974 with the construction of the first phase of The Gallery.

The easiest way to reach the City Hall East area is to take a bus on Market Street or the Market-Frankford subway line to 13th or 15th streets.

Market Street east
1911

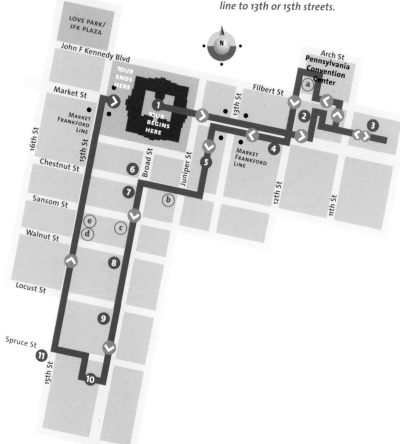

City Hall

1871–1901

Broad and Market streets
John McArthur, Jr., architect,
with Thomas U. Walter

Open to the public

Reading Terminal

1891–93

Market Street,
11th to 12th streets
The Wilson Brothers
renovated 1993-94,
Thompson, Ventulett,
Stainback & Associates,
with the Vitetta Group,
Kelly/Maiello Architects,
Livingston/Rosenwinkel P.C.

Open to the public

The tour begins at City Hall and proceeds along Market Street, then along South Broad Street, returning to the west side of City Hall where it connects to the City Hall West tour.

The first building on the tour is ❶ **City Hall**. City Hall is the largest municipal building in the country and the finest example of the Second Empire style. It contains 14 acres of floor space, occupied by city and county offices, courtrooms and a number of public spaces that are among the most lavish in the city. These include the City Council chamber, the Mayor's Reception Room and Conversation Hall.

City Hall is covered with sculpture, all created by Alexander Milne Calder. Calder also designed the 27-ton cast iron statue of William Penn atop the tower, which is the largest single piece of sculpture on any building in the world. The 491-foot high tower is the world's tallest masonry structure without a steel frame. It is granite up to the clock, then cast iron painted to look like stone.

Tours of the public rooms in City Hall are offered daily. The tower is open to the public and affords a wonderful view of the city.

After visiting City Hall, leave by the east portico and walk along the north side of Market Street to 12th Street to the ❷

Reading Terminal and Pennsylvania Convention Center. *Enter the Convention Center on Market Street just past 12th Street and take the escalator up to the second level.*

When steam locomotives eliminated the fear of fire from wood-burning engines, the Reading Railroad built a new inner-city terminal in 1893 on the site occupied by the Franklin Farmers' Market. The market, now known as the Reading Terminal Market, was given space under the train shed where it remains in operation to this day.

The Head House on Market Street, now a hotel and entry to the Convention Center, originally contained waiting rooms and offices. The train shed is the only surviving single-span arched train shed in the country. It was the largest single-span structure in the world when completed. The shed has been preserved by incorporating it into the Pennsylvania Convention Center. A grand hall, ballroom and meeting rooms are located in the shed, which is connected to a new building to the north containing exhibit space.

Take the escalator back down to street level, turn left and take another escalator down to the lower level. Proceed straight ahead into The Gallery to another set of escalators and take those back up to street level.

❸ **The Gallery** was one of the most ambitious of the mid-20th-century plans for the revitalization of Center City. Although planning began in the late 1950s, it wasn't until 1964 that the city and business community agreed on a plan for a six-block-long skylit pedestrian mall, one level below

The Gallery
1974–77, 1982–83
Market Street between
9th and 11th streets
Bower and Fradley/
Bower Lewis Thrower
and Cope Linder Associates
Open to the public

**Loew's Philadelphia
Hotel**
PSFS Building
1930–32
12 South 12th Street
Howe and Lescaze
renovated 2000,
Bower Lewis Thrower
Open to the public

the street, with retail shops connecting existing department stores at either end. Although only half this ambitious proposal was carried out, The Gallery contains over 130 stores organized around a dramatic, four-story-high, sky-lit space.

Adjacent to The Gallery is the Market East Train Station, created by the construction in 1984 of an underground tunnel linking the Pennsylvania Railroad Suburban Station at 15th Street to a new underground station replacing the Reading Terminal.

After walking around the upper levels of The Gallery, take the escalator back to the lowest level, return along the same route and take the escalator back up to the Convention Center lobby. At the top of the escalator look to the right for the passageway leading to the ⓐ **Reading Terminal Market**. *Go out that exit and cross Filbert Street into the market.*

The farmers' market was saved from elimination in 1892 by being relocated beneath the new train station. Threatened with elimination a second time in 1992 by the construction of the Pennsylvania Convention Center, the market survived, was rebuilt and is now one of the most vibrant and eclectic retail spaces in Center City. Individual merchant stands sell fresh produce, meat, ice cream, baked goods and much more. It's a wonderful place to stop and have lunch.

Leave the Reading Terminal Market by a 12th Street exit, turn left and walk to 12th and Market streets to the ❹ **Loew's Philadelphia Hotel**, originally the **PSFS Building**, one of the most important buildings in the city.

When the Philadelphia Savings Fund Society decided to build a new headquarters, the directors chose a site near the Reading Terminal and Wanamaker's department store, where they already had a successful branch bank. They hired George Howe, a well-known architect of pastoral suburban houses, who entered into partnership with William Lescaze, a Swiss architect. Together they designed the first International style skyscraper in the country.

PSFS is a masterpiece; it is the finest 20th-century building in the city and one of the most important examples of the International Style in the country. The base contained a retail store on the first floor, with the banking room located above. Bank offices above were set back from the facade of the office tower, which rises to a complicated roof structure and a prominent sign. Even though PSFS was built at the height of the Depression, expensive materials and furnishings were used throughout.

When PSFS was converted to the Loew's Philadelphia Hotel, the exterior remained unchanged and most of the important interior spaces were preserved. The most dramatic interior space—the high-ceilinged banking room—was converted to a banquet room.

After visiting the second floor banquet room of the hotel, walk west along Market Street, past 13th Street and enter the ❺ **John Wanamaker Building and Macy's Department Store**.

 5

John Wanamaker Building

Macy's Department Store

1902–11

13th and Market streets
D. H. Burnham and
Company, with
John T. Windrim
renovated 1991,
Ewing Cole Cherry Brott

Open to the public

6

Ritz-Carlton Hotel

Girard Trust Company

1905–08

34–36 S. Broad Street
McKim, Mead and White
renovated 2002, Hillier
Architecture

Open to the public

When John Wanamaker decided to construct a new store, he wanted the existing store to remain in operation. As a result, the building was constructed in three stages, which required considerable care to make sure that the joining of the stages was invisible. The handsome granite and limestone exterior is an adaptation of the Renaissance palace, greatly enlarged in scale. Inside, the selling floors were organized around a spectacular central court that rises five floors. It is the most impressive interior space of any commercial building in the city. The Wanamaker Organ in the Grand Court is the largest musical instrument in the world. Concerts are given daily at noon.

After walking through the Grand Court exit to Chestnut Street, turn right and walk to Broad Street. Note the ⓑ **Keystone National Bank** (1887/1890), 1326 Chestnut Street, a flamboyant design by Willis Hale derived from French chateaux of the Loire Valley.

While retail development dominated Market Street, the completion of City Hall on Center Square in 1901 attracted banks, offices and hotels to South Broad Street. Center Square was set aside for public use by William Penn in the original plan of Philadelphia. Although the site was temporarily used as the site of a Quaker meetinghouse and from 1779 to 1800 for a pump house for the city's waterworks, it was too far on the edge of the developed area of the city to attract interest until the late 1800s. A public referendum in 1870 selected it as the site for a new City Hall. Over the next 40 years, this decision resulted in a gradual shift in the center of government and finance from 6th and Chestnut streets to South Broad Street, where it remained until the 1950s.

At the northwest corner of Broad and Chestnut streets is the **6 Ritz-Carlton Hotel**, originally the **Girard Trust Company**. The Girard Trust building is the city's best example of the Neoclassical style introduced in the United States at the 1893 Columbian Exposition in Chicago. It was designed by Stanford White of McKim, Mead and White, whose firm was responsible for much of the work at the Chicago Exposition, although based on plans prepared by Frank Furness.

With its gleaming white marble walls, handsome portico and distinctive dome, the Girard Trust building has all the characteristics of a classical temple. However, it used modern construction techniques; behind the marble exterior is a steel-frame structure. The adjacent office building, also in white marble, was added in 1923 by McKim, Mead and White. The buildings were converted to the Ritz-Carlton Hotel in 2002, with guest rooms in the former office tower and a magnificent lobby in the former banking room.

Opposite the Ritz-Carlton Hotel is the **7 Land Title Building**.

The Land Title Building is the finest example of early skyscraper design in Philadelphia and the earliest East Coast example of this style by a major Chicago architect. The building has alternating strips of projecting and flat windows, typical of the Chicago Commercial style. The continuous

Land Title Building

1897

Broad and Chestnut streets
D. H. Burnham and
Company

Bellevue Stratford Hotel

1902–13

Broad and Walnut streets
G. W. and W. D. Hewitt
remodeled 1980, 1989
Day and Zimmerman
Associates/ Vitetta Group
with RTKL Architects
Open to the public

Academy of Music

1855–57

232–46 South Broad Street
Napoleon LeBrun and
Gustave Runge

vertical piers, terminating in arches at the top, express the frame and were standard devices used to emphasize the building's height. Although built as a speculative office building, the interiors were finished in expensive materials, including marble and hardwood floors and marble wainscoting in the corridors.

From Chestnut Street, walk south on Broad Street to Locust Street. Along the way are several distinctive buildings. The Ⓒ **Union League** (1864–65), 140 South Broad Street, designed by John Fraser, was one of the many political clubs organized during the Civil War years. The brick and brownstone building, an early example of the Second Empire style, was one of the few buildings erected in Philadelphia during the Civil War.

Further down Broad Street at Walnut Street is the ❽ **Bellevue**, originally the **Bellevue Stratford Hotel**, once the city's most fashionable hotel and still one of its finest. It was designed by G. W. and W. D. Hewitt, two of the most prolific Philadelphia architects of the 19th century. Although the building was constructed of steel in the most modern method, the exterior was inspired by the architectural style of the French Renaissance. Today the Bellevue contains offices, the Park Hyatt Hotel and a number of fine retail stores. The grand rooms—the Grand Ballroom, Rose Garden and lobby—have been preserved and beautifully restored.

The ❾ **Academy of Music** at Broad and Locust streets marks the start of Philadelphia's performing arts district, known as the Avenue of the Arts. This area contains a number of important performing arts facilities as well as the University of the Arts.

Philadelphia's musical development was slow compared with other cities, partly because of the dominant Quaker conservatism. However, by the 1850s the public was eager for opera on a grand scale. A site for a concert hall was acquired on Broad Street, a largely undeveloped, quiet location. The plan, selected by a competition, was modeled after La Scala in Milan. The neo-Baroque interior of the Academy of Music is one of the most lavish in the city. Huge Corinthian columns mark the proscenium and an immense Victorian chandelier hangs from a ceiling decorated with murals by Karl Heinrich Schmolze. The Academy is the oldest musical auditorium in the country still serving its original purpose.

From the Academy of Music continue south to Spruce Street and enter the **10** **Kimmel Center for the Performing Arts.**

In 1990–92, the Central Philadelphia Development Corporation created a plan for a performing arts district along South Broad Street, picking up on an idea first proposed in the 1960s. The plan envisioned a series of performance and arts-related activities extending from the Academy of Music to as far south as Catharine Street. The central feature of the plan was the construction of a new concert hall for the Philadelphia Orchestra. The concert hall was later expanded into the Kimmel Center for the Performing Arts. Beneath a huge, barrel-vaulted glass roof, the Center contains a 2,500-seat concert hall, a 650-seat recital hall and smaller performance spaces and meeting rooms. The separate performance facilities are linked by a dramatic public space and topped by roof gardens.

10

Kimmel Center for the Performing Arts
2001
Broad and Spruce streets
Rafael Viñoly Architects
Open to the public

Exit from the Kimmel Center onto Spruce Street; turn left to 15th Street and then walk north on 15th Street to Market Street and City Hall.

Just west of 15th Street is **11** **The Drake**, one of Center City's most impressive residential buildings. The Drake was one of many tall buildings constructed in Center City in 1929. Even today, its tapered silhouette is a striking feature on the city's skyline. The terra cotta decoration is based on themes related to Sir Francis Drake. Motifs of dolphins, shells, sailing vessels and globes cover the ground floor and reappear on the piers, which rise to an elaborate series of cornices and a distinctive terra cotta dome.

Along 15th Street are a number of other distinctive buildings. At 15th and Walnut streets is the **ⓓ Drexel & Company Building** (1925–27), 135–43 S. 15th Street, based on the design of the Storzzi palace in Florence, Italy. It is a solid fortress of rusticated granite blocks. Immediately north is the **ⓔ addition to the Union League** (1909–11) designed by Horace Trumbauer in a formal Renaissance design that is a startling contrast to the main building on Broad Street.

The tour concludes at Dilworth Plaza on the west side of City Hall, which is where the City Hall West tour begins.

The Drake
1929
1512–1514 Spruce Street
Ritter and Shay
renovated 1998,
VLBJR Architects

City Hall West Tour

As noted in the introduction to the City Hall East tour, Center Square was set aside for public use by William Penn in the original plan of Philadelphia. The selection of Center Square as the site for a new City Hall in 1870 shifted the center of the city away from 6th and Chestnut streets. However, the primary influence on development west of City Hall was the construction of the Pennsylvania Railroad's Broad Street Station in 1881. Its remodeling by Frank Furness in 1889 made it the largest railroad passenger station in the world. Office buildings were constructed adjacent to the station, but commercial development north of Market Street was blocked by the "Chinese Wall" of elevated railroad tracks that extended west to 30th Street Station. Nonetheless, in the early 20th century, West Market Street became the site of the city's grandest movie theaters, all of which have been demolished.

Broad Street Station in 1906

1889

Frank Furness

The demolition of the "Chinese Wall" and construction of a modern office complex over the tracks was one of the ambitious plans of the 1920s. A new suburban train station was completed in 1930, but the demolition of the Chinese Wall and the construction of the office complex—known as Penn Center—did not begin until 1953. Since that time, nearly all new major office buildings have been constructed as part of or adjacent to Penn Center and the underground suburban railroad station.

The easiest way to reach the City Hall west area is to take a bus on Market Street or the Market-Frankford subway line to 15th Street.

The tour begins on the west side of ❶ **City Hall** *in Dilworth Plaza, named for Richardson Dilworth reform mayor of Philadelphia from 1956–1962. For information about City Hall see page 67. After visiting City Hall cross 15th Street to the* ❷ **Penn Center Complex** *and walk through the center pedestrian way.*

Penn Center

1953–82

15th to 18th streets,
between Market Street and
John F. Kennedy Boulevard
Vincent G. Kling and
Assoc./ Emery Roth and
Sons/Kohn Pederson Fox;
renovations 1989, 1986,
Ueland Junker McCauley

In 1953, the Broad Street Station and "Chinese Wall" of elevated railroad tracks behind it were demolished to make way for the city's first new office buildings since the Depression. When the Pennsylvania Railroad proposed demolition of the Broad Street Station, Edmund Bacon, executive director of the Planning Commission, and architect Vincent G. Kling presented a proposal for development of the site. The centerpiece of their plan was a lower level pedestrian area, open to the sky, that connected the subway station and suburban train station with new shops and office buildings. The Railroad accepted some of their ideas, including a series of courtyards to let light into the underground pedestrian area, but adopted a more conventional overall plan of office buildings around a street-level pedestrian way.

Penn Center was the start of the post-war transformation of Center City. It was significant not for the design of the individual buildings, but for the project as a whole. It acted as a catalyst for the development of public open space around City Hall and the construction of the Municipal Services Building nearby; it continues to influence the location of new office buildings even to this day.

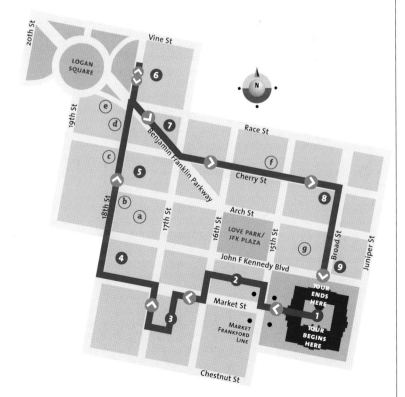

Continue through Penn Center to 16th Street and cross to the south side of Market Street and go right. Turn left in the middle of the block into ❸ **Liberty Place**.

When new office buildings were developed west of City Hall in the 1950s, an informal "gentlemen's agreement" limited their height to no greater than the 491-foot height of City Hall tower, thereby enabling the statue of William Penn atop the tower to preside symbolically over the city. Developer Willard Rouse's proposal to build an office building higher sparked controversy and extensive public debate.

Rouse's One Liberty Place, at a height of 960 feet to the top of its spire, became the tallest building in the city and the most prominent landmark day or night. The 61-story tower has a silver-blue aluminum grid, which holds horizontal bands of blue glass and gray granite at the corners. The central portion of the facade is silver metallic glass. This combination of silver and blue glass gives the building a shimmering quality and delicacy in spite of its massive size. The top of the building, sheathed entirely in glass, is formed

Liberty Place

1987–90

1650 Market Street
Murphy/Jahn and the
Zeidler Roberts Partnership.

Mellon Center

1990

1735 Market Street
Kohn Pederson Fox

Bell Atlantic Tower

1991

17th and Arch streets
The Kling-Lindquist
Partnership

by the repetitive use of a gable form, resulting in a silhouette reminiscent of the Chrysler Building. Linear bands of light along the gable edges give the building a striking presence on the skyline at night.

Two Liberty Place uses the same architectural vocabulary, but in a more subdued fashion. One and Two Liberty Place are connected by an elegant two-story arcade of retail stores. Corner entrances lead to a glass-enclosed rotunda surrounded by two levels of shops and a large food court.

Exit on to 17th Street, turn right to Market Street, then cross to the north side of the street and turn left to the ❹ **Mellon Center**.

Mellon Center, the second building to exceed the height of the City Hall tower, is a 53-story office tower in the form of a gigantic, freestanding obelisk on axis with the tower of City Hall. A lattice, pyramidal structure, housing the building's cooling system, tops the tower and completes the obelisk analogy. A public winter garden for exhibits and displays is housed in a small glass structure between the tower and an older office building.

Continue along Market Street to 18th Street, turn right and walk north on 18th Street to Arch Street. East of 18th Street on John F. Kennedy Boulevard is the site of the 975-foot-high (a) **Comcast Tower** (under construction in 2007), designed by Robert A. M. Stern Architects. It will be the tallest building in Philadelphia when completed in 2008.

At the corner of 18th and Arch streets is the (b) **Arch Street Presbyterian Church** (1853–55), 1724 Arch Street, Joseph C. Hoxie. The church has a copper dome influenced by the design for St. Paul's Cathedral in London. The sanctuary is a masterpiece of the Classical Revival style and one of the most beautiful interiors in the city.

Directly across the street is the **5 Bell Atlantic Tower**. The Bell Atlantic Tower is a contrast to its predecessors in almost every way. Because the site is bisected by the special design controls along the Benjamin Franklin Parkway, which limit the height of buildings, the office tower was placed on the southern edge of the site and designed with stepped-back corners to avoid the line of controls.

Warm red granite accented by honed granite spandrels up the center of the broad facades, gives the building a more sedate and dignified character than One Liberty Place or Mellon Center. Although the tower lacks the dramatic impact of its predecessors, the choice of materials and simplicity of form give the building a refined grace and elegance on the Philadelphia skyline.

6

Cathedral of SS. Peter and Paul

1846–64

18th and Race streets
Napoleon LeBrun and John Notman
Open to the public

From the Bell Atlantic Tower walk north along 18th Street to the Benjamin Franklin Parkway passing (c) **Two Logan Square**, (1984–87), 100 N. 18th Street, (d) **One Logan Square** (1982–83) and the (e) **Four Seasons Hotel** (1982–83), all designed by the Kohn Pederson Fox. The Four Seasons Hotel and One Logan Square is an elegant building complex and one of the first in the city designed in the Postmodern style.

Continue along 18th Street and cross the Benjamin Franklin Parkway to the **6 Cathedral of SS. Peter and Paul**.

Although Catholics had always been present in the city, their numbers were not significant until after the Irish immigration in the 1830s. By 1844, the Irish population was large enough to support the building of a cathedral. The cathedral is the oldest building on Logan Square, one of the original five squares set aside for public use by William Penn. It was one of the most sumptuous churches in the country when completed. The interior is designed in a grand Italian Renaissance style. Notable features include the domed baldachino over the altar, the giant Corinthian pilasters encircling the nave and transept and the deeply coffered barrel vault over the nave. The dome and the elegant brownstone facade were added after 1850.

Return to the Parkway and walk towards City Hall, passing the **❼ United Way Building**, *between 17th and 18th streets.*

❼

United Way Building

1969

Parkway, between 17th and 18th streets
Mitchell/Giurgola Associates

The design controls for the Parkway are intended to ensure that buildings east of 18th Street create a narrow urban space. The United Fund Building is responsive to the intent of the Parkway controls and its urban context.

The small, seven-story structure conforms to its trapezoidal site. Each elevation responds to the unique conditions of its orientation. The north side is a curtain wall of gray-tinted glass, the west wall is shielded from the sun by horizontal concrete sunscreens while allowing views of Logan Square. The south wall, of structural concrete, has deeply recessed windows that block the south sunlight.

At 17th Street and the Parkway, turn left on Cherry Street and continue for three blocks to Broad Street. Along the way is the **ⓕ Race Street Meetinghouse** (1856–57), 1515 Cherry Street. The Quaker meetinghouse was designated a National Historic Landmark in 1992 for its members' active role in supporting women's suffrage.

At the corner of Broad and Cherry streets is the **❽ Pennsylvania Academy of the Fine Arts**. The academy,

❽

Pennsylvania Academy of the Fine Arts

1872–76

Broad and Cherry streets
Furness and Hewitt
restored 1976, Day and Zimmerman Associates
Open to the public

founded in 1805, was the first art school and museum in the country. Its most famous student was Thomas Eakins, who became a dominating presence as a teacher from 1876–86. The academy is the most outstanding example of the work of Frank Furness and one of the most magnificent Victorian buildings in the country. The exterior is an amalgam of historical styles, fused in an aggressively personal manner. The pointed arches, floral ornament and use of color are derived from English Gothic design, while the mansard roof, projecting central pavilion and panels of incised tryglyphs come from French sources.

The interior, in contrast to the somber tones of previous Victorian architecture, is an explosion of color: the walls have gilt floral patterns incised on a field of Venetian red; the cerulean blue ceiling is sprinkled with silver stars; the gallery walls are plum, ochre, sand and olive green.

For many decades the academy was considered to be an unattractive building and its ornamental brilliance was obscured. A comprehensive restoration in 1976 returned the building to its original, extraordinary appearance.

From the Pennsylvania Academy walk south on Broad Street toward City Hall. On the west side of the street is the **ⓖ Municipal Services Building,** (1962–65), Vincent G. Kling and Associates. On the east side is the **❾ Masonic Temple.**

Freemasonry prospered in Philadelphia from colonial times. Several temples were built, culminating in this magnificent structure, one of the world's greatest Masonic temples.

❾

Masonic Temple
1868–73/1890s
1 North Broad Street
James Windrim and
George Herzog
Open to the public

The Masons held a competition and selected Brother James Windrim, a 27-year-old Freemason, as the winner. Windrim's design was modeled on a medieval style known as Norman. This is reflected in the massive carved doorway that projects from the wall; the fortress-like towers; and the round-arch decorated cornice under the roofline.

The temple took five years to build. The interior design was begun 14 years later and took 15 more years to complete. George Herzog, who had trained in the royal workshops of Ludwig I of Munich, was the primary designer. The spectacular interior spaces include seven lodge halls, each lavishly decorated in a specific style. The most renowned is the Egyptian Hall, replete with accurate hieroglyphics. The temple was one of the first buildings in the city to be lighted by electricity. The public entrance for tours of the Masonic Temple is located on the south side of the building opposite City Hall.

To end the City Hall tour, cross the street and return to the City Hall courtyard through the north portico. Inside the portico on the left is a plaque inscribed with the prayer William Penn wrote for Philadelphia when he was leaving Pennsylvania to return to England in 1684.

The tour concludes at City Hall.

The Benjamin Franklin Parkway Tour

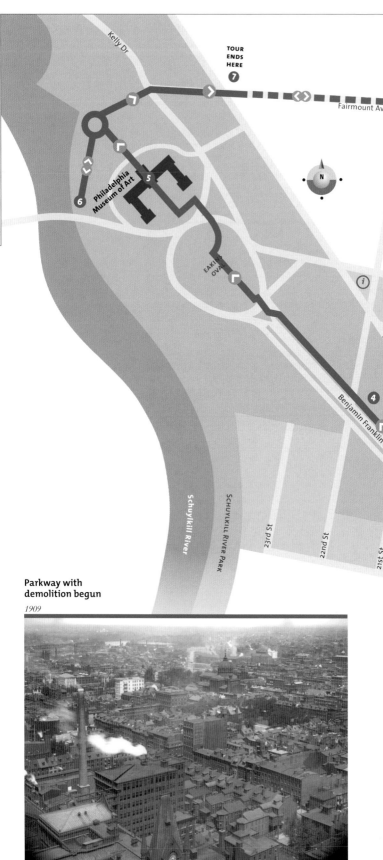

TOUR ENDS HERE

7

8

Kelly Dr

Fairmount Ave

N

7

6

Philadelphia Museum of Art

5

EAKINS OVAL

i

Spring

Hamilt

Pennsylvania Ave

4

Benjamin Franklin Parkway

Schuylkill River

SCHUYLKILL RIVER PARK

23rd St

22nd St

21st St

h

20th St

Race St

Parkway with demolition begun

1909

The idea of a diagonal parkway from Center Square to Fairmount Park was first proposed in 1884 and again in 1891, when it gained sufficient support to be placed on the city map. But the parkway proposal languished until 1902 when a group of prominent civic leaders formed the Parkway Association to promote the idea. It was placed back on the city plan in 1903 and acquisition and demolition of property west of Logan Square began in 1907. By 1915, 1,300 buildings had been demolished to make way for the new boulevard.

Originally the parkway was to terminate at Faire Mount, the site of the city reservoir. But by 1907 it was determined that the reservoir on Faire Mount was no longer needed. Supporters of a new art museum, who had been looking for an appropriate site since 1883, suggested Faire Mount as the site for the museum and linked it to the parkway plan. The idea received strong support from Mayor John Reyburn. At the time, the concept of diagonal boulevards cutting across the grid plan of the city was very popular, not only in Philadelphia, but also in such other cities as Chicago and Washington, D.C., influenced in part by the 1893 Columbian Exposition in Chicago. The Exposition introduced European ideas about planning and architecture to the American public and created the impetus for the City Beautiful movement, the first American contribution to modern city planning. The Parkway in Philadelphia was one of its principal examples.

After the idea of a new museum and the parkway were combined, the Fairmount Park Art Association responded by commissioning prominent architect Paul Philippe Cret in collaboration with others to produce a plan that unified the two ideas. Later, in 1917, the Fairmount Park Commission, which had recently been given jurisdiction over the Parkway, commissioned French planner Jacques Greber to review Cret's plans. Greber revised the plans, drawing on the Champs Elysées in Paris as his inspiration, including modeling the design for Logan Square after the Place de La Concorde and changing its name to Logan Circle. Although Greber's plan was modified as the Parkway came to function as a major transportation artery, his plan set the character of the Parkway as it is today. In recent years, the Parkway has been enhanced by the lighting of major buildings and monuments and improvements to public spaces.

The Parkway was opened in 1918; however all the major civic buildings—the Art Museum, Free Library, Franklin Institute and Municipal Court— were not completed until 1941. The Parkway was named after Benjamin Franklin in 1937. Today it is the site of public festivals and parades.

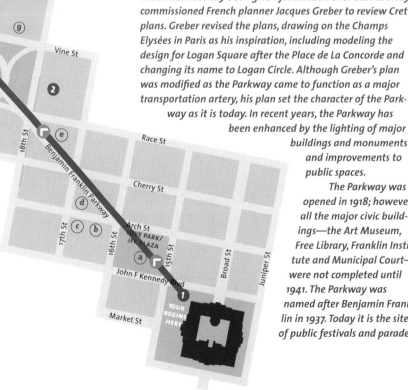

The tour of the Parkway begins at Dilworth Plaza on the west side of ❶ **City Hall**. The plaza is named after Mayor Richardson Dilworth (1956–62) whose leadership was instrumental in starting the transformation of Center City. A description of City Hall is included at the start of the City Hall East tour on page 77.

After visiting City Hall return to the northwest corner and look northwest along the Parkway to the Philadelphia Museum of Art in the distance. It is one mile from City Hall to the museum. The tour can be taken as a walking tour, or as a walking tour to Logan Square and then by bus to the Art Museum.

From the northwest corner of City Hall cross 15th Street and then cross Kennedy Boulevard into ⓐ **Love Park**. The park, built on top of an underground parking garage, was constructed in the 1960s as part of the plan developed around the new Penn Center office complex. It is named after the *Love* sculpture by Robert Indiana on the upper level of the park on axis with the Parkway. At the entrance to Love Park is an historic marker commemorating Edmund Bacon and his contributions to Philadelphia planning.

Walk through Love Park to the Parkway and cross Arch Street and then 16th Street and then proceed along the Parkway to Logan Circle.

The first major building on the Parkway is ⓑ **The Phoenix**, 1600 Arch Street, formerly the **Insurance Company of North America**, (1925), Stewardson and Page. The company was organized in 1792. Its Georgian Revival headquarters was one of the earliest buildings constructed along the Parkway. It is one of the many historic office buildings in Center City converted to residential use following the creation of a ten-year tax abatement program in 1997. To the west at 17th and Arch streets is the ⓒ **INA Annex**, a sleek, pale-green aluminum addition, completed in 1979 by Mitchell/Giurgola Associates. Nearby is the ⓓ **Bell Telephone Company** (1916), designed by John T. Windrim. It was the first private building constructed along the new parkway.

Further along the Parkway past 17th Street is the ⓔ **United Way Building**, also designed by Mitchell/Giurgola Associates and described on page 86. The Bell Telephone Company building, The Phoenix and the United Way Building reflect the influence of the special design controls that were adopted for the Parkway. These require all buildings from 16th Street to 18th Street to be built to the street line to create a narrow, urban connection from Logan Square to City Hall. By contrast, past 20th Street the design controls require all buildings to be set back to preserve the landscape character of the Parkway as far as the Art Museum.

Continue to 18th Street and cross over into the center of ⓕ **Logan Square**. This was one of the original five squares set aside for public use by William Penn in the original plan of the city. Initially called Northwest Square, it was a site of public executions and burial plots until the early 19th century. The central circular form was created in the 1920s as part of the development of the Parkway. It contains the Swann Fountain, designed by Alexander Sterling Calder, son of the Alexander Milne Calder who created the statue of William Penn on top of City Hall tower. The three reclining figures represent the three rivers of Philadelphia: the Delaware, Schuylkill and Wissahickon.

The first building constructed on Logan Square was ❷ **the Cathedral of SS Peter and Paul**. (See the City Hall West tour page 85 for a description.) The two buildings to the north—the ❸ **Free Library** and ⓖ **Family Court Building**—

were both conceived as part of the Parkway plan. Since the Parkway was modeled after the Champs Elysées in Paris it was logical for the two buildings to be modeled after the twin palaces on the Place de la Concorde in Paris, which occupied a similar position on the boulevard. The Free Library was designed by Horace Trumbauer, but probably heavily influenced by Julian Abele, Trumbauer's chief designer, who had made recent trips to Paris. Abele was the first black graduate of the University of Pennsylvania School of Architecture. When completed, the Library was one of the largest and most modern in the world. It was considered the ultimate in fireproof construction.

Free Library
1917–27

Vine Street, between 19th and 20th streets
Horace Trumbauer
Open to the public

The ⓖ **Municipal Court Building** (1938–41), designed by John T. Windrim, now **Family Court**, is adjacent to and matches the Free Library. Its construction was financed in part by the federal Works Progress Administration (WPA). Within the building are stained glass designs by the D'Ascenzo Studios and paintings by nine artists, sponsored by the Public Works Administration.

On the far side of Logan Square is the ⓗ **Franklin Institute** (1931–34), also designed by John T. Windrim. The building contains a central rotunda with a huge marble statue of Benjamin Franklin. Only half of the original design was built, allowing the Institute's Mandell Futures Center and an Imax theater to be added in 1990, adjacent to the Fels Planetarium.

❹

Rodin Museum
1927–29

Parkway and 22nd Street
Paul Philippe Cret and
Jacques Greber
Open to the public

Continue along the Parkway to 22nd Street and the ❹ **Rodin Museum** *or, in summer, take the Phlash bus from in front of the Free Library to the Art Museum.*

The Rodin Museum houses the largest collection of Auguste Rodin's work outside France. The gateway to the museum is a replica of the Chateau d'Issy, reconstructed by Rodin for his own home in Meudon, France. Several of Rodin's most popular sculptures are incorporated into the architectural composition including *The Thinker* and *The Gates of Hell*, the bronze doors at the entrance to the museum.

After passing the Rodin Museum in the distance to the right is ⓘ **Parkway House**, (1952–53), 22nd Street and Pennsylvania Avenue, Gabriel Roth and Elizabeth Fleisher, architects. Parkway House, one of the first postwar luxury apartment buildings in the city, is an exceptionally fine design with elements from both the Art Deco and International styles. The building is also noteworthy because it was one of the first in the city designed by a woman architect.

At the end of the Parkway, cross over to Eakins Oval, proceed around the statue of George Washington and cross the street at the light to the grand flight of stairs that leads to the ❺ **Philadelphia Museum of Art**. Entrance to the museum by public transportation is from the west side of the building.

Initial plans for the museum were prepared separately

by Trumbauer and by Zantzinger and Borie. Julian Abele, Trumbauer's chief designer, returned from Greece with the idea of building three temples on a solid rock base. However, the final design appears to have been a compromise among all their ideas worked out by Howell Lewis Shay, an architect in Trumbauer's office.

At the start of construction, not enough money had been raised to build the entire building. Eli Kirk Price, one of the fundraisers, suggested building the two wings first, on the correct presumption that Philadelphians would not leave the museum unfinished.

The museum is constructed of warm, yellow Minnesota Mankato and Kosota ashlar on the facade with a gabled blue tile roof. In addition to its outstanding art collection, the museum contains a number of rooms representing different architectural periods, most of which were built as WPA projects during the 1930s. They include a Japanese teahouse and a Chinese temple.

After visiting the museum leave by the west entrance and walk down the grand stairs to the Italian fountain, then turn left and walk along the Schuylkill River to the ❻ **Fairmount Water Works**.

Philadelphia Museum of Art

1916–1928

Benjamin Franklin Parkway and 26th Street
Horace Trumbauer,
C. Clark Zantzinger,
Charles L. Borie, Jr.
Open to the public

Fairmount Water Works

1812–15

Fairmount, at Schuylkill River near 25th Street
Frederick Graff
Open to the public

The first city water works were located on Center Square. When a new system was required, it was moved to the Schuylkill River. It was one of the most notable engineering accomplishments of its day. The original steam pumping station carried nearly four million gallons of water every day from the river to the reservoir at the top of Faire Mount where the Art Museum is now located. The complex, added to throughout the 19th century, was modeled after Roman temples and arranged around paved courts and walkways. It was one of the most popular sights with visitors to the city in the 19th century, including British author Charles Dickens. Today the Engine House contains a fine restaurant. In the basement is a museum operated by the Philadelphia Water Department

Ruth and Raymond G. Perelman Building

Fidelity Mutual Life Insurance Company

1925–26

Pennsylvania and Fairmount avenues
Zantzinger, Borie and Medary
renovated 2006–2007, Gluckman Mayner Architects

Open to the public

that describes the history of the city's water supply system.

From the Water Works walk back to the Italian fountain, then bear to the right and continue to Kelly Drive. Cross Kelly Drive to the **7** **Perelman Building**, originally the **Fidelity Mutual Life Insurance Building**.

The Fidelity Mutual Life Insurance Building was planned in conjunction with the Parkway. In contrast to the Parkway's classical civic buildings, the Fidelity Building was designed in the Art Deco style, popular for commercial buildings in the 1920s and 1930s. The building integrates sculpture and decoration typical of the period around the two massive arched portals, the window spandrels and the cornice. The Fidelity Building was renamed, extensively restored and expanded by the Philadelphia Museum of Art in 2006–07 to provide new galleries and administrative space for the museum.

Although not part of the story of the Benjamin Franklin Parkway, **8** **Eastern State Penitentiary** is only a few blocks from the Perelman Building. It was one of the most influential Philadelphia buildings in the 19th century and is worth a side trip.

If not visiting Eastern State return to the west entrance of the Art Museum for public transportation back to City Hall. To visit Eastern State, proceed along Fairmount Avenue to its entrance near 22nd Street.

Eastern State Penitentiary

1823–36

Fairmount Avenue and 21st Street
John Haviland

Open to the public

Early Quakers believed that criminals could be reformed by placing them in solitary confinement to contemplate their past deeds and seek divine guidance. Eastern State was based on this philosophy. The original plan consisted of seven long cellblocks radiating from a central surveillance rotunda. Each cellblock contained individual solitary cells and work yards. The cellblocks and prison yard were enclosed behind a massive stone wall with square towers flanking the entrance and battlemented turrets at the corners. The design was enormously influential and copied by more than 500 prisons around the world.

Up to its closing in 1972, buildings were steadily added, obscuring the original plan. Some famous prisoners stayed here, including the bank robber Willie Sutton. After being vacant for 16 years and threatened with demolition, concerned citizens began to offer tours. Since 1996, the nonprofit Eastern State Penitentiary Historic Site has managed the building, restored many parts of it and organized a number of fascinating art installations.

Bibliography

Bacon, Edmund N.
Design of Cities.
New York: Viking, 1967.

Brownlee, David B.
Building the City Beautiful.
Philadelphia: The Philadelphia Museum of Art,
1989.

Central Philadelphia Development Corporation.
**OPDC/CPDC: A History of the Central Philadelphia
Development Corporation**.
Philadelphia: CPDC, 2006.

Farnham, Jonathan E.
**"A Bridge Game: Constructing a Cooperative Common-
wealth in Philadelphia, 1900-1926."**
Doctoral Dissertation, School of Architecture,
Princeton University, 2007.

Gallery, John Andrew, ed.
Philadelphia Architecture, A Guide to the City,
2nd Edition.
Philadelphia: Foundation for Architecture, 1994.

Gallery, John Andrew, ed.
Philadelphia's Best Buildings In (and Near) Center City.
Philadelphia: Foundation for Architecture, 1994.

Gallery, John Andrew.
**William Penn's Plan of Philadelphia and the Early
Growth of the City**.
Unpublished manuscript © 2004.

Philadelphia *Evening Bulletin*.

Temple University Urban Archives.

Roach, Hannah Benner.
**"The Planting of Philadelphia: A Seventeenth-Century
Real Estate Development."**
The Pennsylvania Magazine of History and
Biography, Volume XCII, Number 1, January 1968
and Number 2, April 1968.

Wallace, David A.
"Renaissancemanship."
Journal of American Institute of Planners,
Volume XXVI, Number 3, August 1960.

Weigley, Russell, ed.
Philadelphia: A 300-Year History.
New York: W.W. Norton & Co., 1982.

Index